P9-CKC-835

Crossing the Line

DANICA PATRICK

WITH LAURA MORTON

A FIRESIDE BOOK
PUBLISHED BY SIMON & SCHUSTER
NEW YORK   LONDON   TORONTO   SYDNEY

FIRESIDE
Rockefeller Center
1230 Avenue of the Americas
New York, NY 10020

For information regarding special discounts for bulk purchases,
please contact Simon & Schuster Special Sales at
1-800-456-6798 or business@simonandschuster.com.

Designed by Elliott Beard

Manufactured in the United States of America

1   3   5   7   9   10   8   6   4   2

Library of Congress Catalog Card Number: 2006044423

ISBN-13: 978-0-7432-9814-8
ISBN-10: 0-7432-9814-4

This book is dedicated to my mom, dad,
sister, and husband for always being there for me

Contents

Contents

Foreword

Bobby Rahal

I first read about Danica Patrick in various karting magazines. I like to follow young drivers who show promise and potential. Danica was no exception. Many of the drivers she was racing against were considered the nation's best, several of whom were expected to move up in their careers and succeed internationally. One of the most important things I look for in a driver is a desire to be a big fish in a big pond—not a big fish in a little pond. That is Danica Patrick.

Though I knew her name, I didn't meet Danica until September 2000. We were introduced by the Ford Motor people. Ford was one of Danica's sponsors in England, and at the time my team was the factory Ford team in IndyCar racing. I was about to leave for England to run the Jaguar Formula One team, which was also owned by Ford. The weekend we first met, I mentioned to Danica that I get over to England every now and then and when I do, I'd give her a call to get together. I knew I'd be able to keep in touch with Danica from time to time and in the process I would be able to monitor her progress. The first time I went to England to race, I was twenty-five years old— Danica was just a teenager when she went through the program. My recollection of competing there is that it was a very lonely existence. I understood the difficult situations she faced daily as a young driver, especially during her years in England. It is a rough and challenging experience.

Danica's career was one of stops and starts. While there was a lot of interest in her, it seemed to me the interest being shown by other teams was genuine but they hadn't really thought about what kind of commitment it was going to take to bring Danica along as a driver. The stop-and-go nature of her career was a reflection of the lack of commitment by teams and owners. While we were both in England, I offered her a test in a Jaguar Formula Three car, which was logical as she was a Ford driver and we were a Ford team. I thought it would be a good experience for her and would give her the opportunity to show the rest of the world what I saw in her from the very start. Unfortunately, politics reared its head and Ford had no interest in pursuing Danica for Formula Three—and I suppose for Formula One by extension. Though she had done extremely well in England, placing second in the Formula Ford Festival in 2000, this wasn't enough to garner the support of the old boys club of racing in England. For better or worse, racing is about champions—it's about aligning your team with the people who are going to beat the drums *for* you. It doesn't matter how good you are or could be, the opportunities are few and far between without a proven track record.

After an especially bad 2000 racing season, I returned to the United States around the same time Danica did. We stayed in touch, talking every now and then. I tried to give Danica every opportunity I could to help her find a ride. Though I don't think Danica knew it at the time, she didn't have to work that hard to get my commitment or faith in her as a driver. She already had it. Signing Danica as a driver was an easy decision for me. She had continuously proven to me something all drivers have to prove before I'll sign them — that they will do whatever it takes or go wherever they need to go in order to achieve their dreams and goals. Danica survived England, which is an extremely competitive environment, one that is difficult for a strong, confident young man; for a young woman, it is almost impossibly difficult. There had been other women who had raced there before Danica, but it's a hostile environment at best. That she was willing to compete there and endure all of the challenges of racing under those circumstances, showed me that Danica was very certain about what she wanted and would stop at nothing to achieve it.

Her talent was obvious. Her commitment is what really spoke to me. There are a lot of talented people in this world who don't have the mental discipline or determination that Danica has. It's why she excels and succeeds. But, unlike many women before her, Danica has something the others have lacked — the commitment of a strong team supporting her and backing her every step of the way. A lot of people say they want to win; few actually show it. Danica proves to me every day how much she wants to succeed. That perseverance is what makes the heart of a champion.

Danica has that chip on her shoulder that all champion drivers need to make it. She's not fearful or unwilling to face any challenge. She not only wants the challenge, she looks for it. That's what champions do. They are not afraid and they don't shy from difficult times. They go through life with a bring-it-on attitude. And it is that "C'mon, take a shot at me" thinking that spurs her confidence and allows her to sustain a challenge and come back harder. It's what I call fire in the belly. It's a hunger and need to be the best. That is Danica.

Foreword

I think Danica gets a lot of her drive from her dad, TJ. She has been fortunate that her parents did whatever they needed to do to support Danica's ambition. Her father is very demanding, which has been a good thing for Danica over the years. She grew up with someone expecting something from her. He pushed hard to see her succeed, and Danica was able to reap the benefits of his ambition and expectations. As a team owner, my expectations are less emotional than that of a parent, but my depth of expectation is probably greater. I've staked my name and reputation on Danica, a risk well worth taking. She has never let me down. When I first put her in the Toyota Atlantic Series, I told people she could drive and deliver—and she did. When I suggested we move her up to IndyCars, despite a lot of people wondering why I chose to bump her up, I knew she could face the task and meet it with skill and great determination. She did. I was willing to gamble on Danica because I knew she was willing to give back more than we gave and also determined and committed to deliver her best effort each and every race. She always rises to the occasion. She may not have won races, but she continued to be fiercely competitive, undaunted by her performance, remaining serious and bringing her extraordinary devotion and work ethic to the sport and track every time she drives. When somebody consistently does that, it's not hard to continue giving her my support.

In every driver's life, there is a moment that changes everything. Even though I had won many races before, in the 1986 Indy 500, with 3 laps to go, I was driving second when I had the opportunity to pass the leader and I went on to win the race. My career skyrocketed from that day on. In life, there is always a moment of truth. If you respond and act on it, you go on. If you don't, you never get the chance again.

The way Danica responded after driving Toyota Atlantic and, of course, after her phenomenal races in Motegi, Japan, and the Indy 500, I knew she was born to be a champ. Though I didn't expect things to happen quite at the pace they did, I knew her moment of truth was upon us. She was ready, willing, and able—her time had come.

I started Danica's 2005 IRL season by telling her I didn't care where she finished, she could be last or first, all I expected was that she finished races. She needed time on the track—something she hadn't had a lot of when she started the season. As her comfort level grew on the track, so did her confidence and performance. Every time she succeeded, she built her own self-belief that she could not only compete but also that she could win. Danica can drive fast—but driving in the pressure-packed situation of a race is different from driving fast during practice or qualifying. She set lofty goals for herself. There were times I may have worried or thought they were too ambitious for her level of experience. I never wanted her to be let down or have unrealistic expectations. Too much disappointment could set back any driver. Every rookie driver has to take his or her first season step by step. It's a learning experience. As a team owner, all I can hope for is that my drivers continue to improve with every race. Danica took those steps at a faster pace than most, but that's Danica. There is nothing ordinary or conventional about this woman. As time went on, she impressed a lot of people. She drove her car way beyond other drivers of the same chassis. Even the other drivers were beginning to understand and acknowledge what I knew from the start—Danica is the real deal.

As the sole woman on the track, the media expectations of Danica

Foreword

Patrick far exceed that of the regular Indy driver. She has to prove herself just a little more than the guys do. Her life, her career, her performance, and her track record are all open to a kind of scrutiny and debate that other drivers simply haven't had to face. Male or female, there is no substitute for talent. Danica handled the pressure with dignity and grace on every level. Right or wrong, fair or unfair, Danica knows and accepts her responsibility with the same level of confidence in which she drives.

Being a woman in this extremely male-oriented sport has had a huge impact on the sport. There is no doubt that her presence in the IRL has brought a new fan base to the sport. Not just young girls who have their own aspirations of someday driving like Danica but also older fans who love this young girl on the track beating the boys. She has brought back fans that have left the sport, repairing the rift between CART and Indy and in the process, Danica has created new opportunities for fans and drivers alike to enjoy the rising popularity of Indy racing. Her influence has been tremendously positive. Her story is so compelling because she is doing what only a few have done before her—she is driving race cars professionally and is poised to win many races in the future.

Every driver needs a champion—someone who rallies behind him and makes other people believe in him. I have watched Danica Patrick grow and mature both on and off the track. Being her champion is easy for me—I have a sense of pride in her that makes me proud both as her boss and as her friend and mentor. What you see is what you get. With all the attention focused on Danica, she skillfully managed to balance her driving and performance on the track and the tremendous pressure she endures off the track in ways that make me very proud. Not only did her driving come of age but Danica came of age. The best part of having Danica on my team is that she gives us a chance to win. That's what racing is all about. She has already proven she is competitive—it's only a matter of time before she grabs the checkered flag. One year later, I suspect Danica mania hasn't waned—I hope it never will. My greatest satisfaction comes from seeing Danica do what she has spent her young life dreaming about—racing cars. She's exciting to watch, a pleasure to know, and a true winner to her core.

Danica—Crossing the Line

Introduction

Trust thy dreams, for in them is hidden the gate to eternity.

—Kahlil Gibran

The dreams were always the same. I was running as fast as I could, trying to escape the wolves that were chasing me. I ran and ran and ran, sweat pouring from my forehead, dripping into my eyes, stinging them as if a thousand bees had attacked me, leaving me blind. And still, I ran. I ran as fast as I could, trying to escape, but then I became stuck, unable to move. My mouth was open, as if I were yelling, but silence emerged. I was unable to scream, to yell for help. I was paralyzed—filled with fear.

Motegi, Japan, 2005

This was my first time visiting Japan, and I was very excited. It wasn't just the anticipation of the race. It was great seeing Tokyo and the country of Japan. I know that I came to Motegi as a rookie, but this

Introduction

track was different than the others I had run prior to coming here to race. Each end of the track is different; one end is really fast and wide, and the other end is much tighter. I hoped to do well here. My teammates Buddy Rice and Vitor Meira have both raced at Motegi before, so they gave me some tips and advice on what to expect.

Clear skies and bright sunshine greeted the racers and the enthusiastic fans on race day. Motegi is a world-class 1.5-mile oval track. It was a pretty solid opening day for me. It took me some time to get up to speed, but my team made some good changes to my car in each of the two practice sessions, and we were able to work on both the qualifying and race day setups. It was a little hotter than I expected, which meant we had to adjust the car from the initial setup because of the changed conditions. I am getting more used to the faster oval tracks. Every time I race, I learn a little more about driving an IndyCar, and this race would be the biggest lesson so far. There is a wealth of talent and experience in this series, which means there's no room for anyone to view me as a fluke, or just another woman trying to race cars. I was beginning to show the improvement everyone looks for from rookies, and it felt good that other people were starting to see my skill shine through.

After a couple of races of qualifying at the back of the pack, I finally qualified in the top two, losing the much-sought-after and coveted pole position to Sam Hornish by 0.002 of a second. He edged me out after I led the qualifying race for most of the day. This field was as tight and competitive as it has been all season. I was uncertain how qualifying would go. I wasn't sure if I could win the pole, but after the first lap, the car felt good—really good. After my qualification attempt, I kept looking over my shoulder at the scoring tower to see if anyone had beaten my time. The conditions got a little cooler with the onset of some cloud cover, which worked to Sam's benefit, and I was bumped to "P2"—second place.

Finally, after three prior races of qualifying slow, I suddenly understood what it felt like to start on the front row of an Indy Racing League (IRL) race. It was awesome. It felt as if a ton of bricks had been lifted from my shoulders. Maybe it was that proverbial "rookie" weight that had been slowing me down up to this race. It didn't matter. I knew I had arrived as a driver, and it felt great. I was nervous. This was the first time I had started in the front, and I knew it was my first real chance of the season to show these boys what I was made of . . . and it's not sugar and spice. Nope. Not this girl. I was filled with adrenaline and determination, piss and vinegar.

I took the lead right from the start, passing Sam on the outside at turn two. I nearly spun in the middle of the pass. My tires were cold, which means they didn't have much grip on the track. But I managed to make it stick and took the lead. I was in the lead for a while, being chased by the other drivers as if they were those wolves that used to haunt me in my dreams. But this chase was no dream. It was real. It was happening live, in full Technicolor, and at 220 mph. I realized that day I am no longer terrified of being chased. In fact, I love being chased. It meant I was in the lead. I raced in front for most of the day—and I felt relieved.

Racing experts say that if you have a good race in Motegi, chances are you'll have a good race in Indianapolis. I wasn't sure if that was true or not. All I knew was that I was having the time of my life. But I was disappointed by the outcome. My engineer gave me the direction to change fuel positions, which restricts the amount of fuel going through the engine. If I hadn't conserved my fuel by slowing down, I would never have made it to the finish line. This strategy got me my highest finishing position so far. It was a challenging race because I am learning I can't always drive the car as hard as I would like—and I like to drive hard. I gained precious experience, which is what a rookie season is all about. It was frustrating, because the car was so good. I started second and finished fourth—things were looking up.

There was no turning back. I now had the confirmation that I could be a real contender in racing. Other people now knew it too. I showed the doubters I can lead a race, set the pace, and possibly—no, probably—find an IRL win. Though nobody ever said it to my face, prior to Motegi I think a lot of people were skeptical of my ability. They thought I was a good publicity tool for the IRL but never gave me the respect or credit I deserved as a driver—at least not until *that* day.

The chase was officially "on" after that race. I knew I had a shot at winning the Indy 500, and now so did everyone else.

What's mine is mine and what's your is up for grabs.

—*Anonymous*

Roscoe, Illinois, 1992

Most young girls aren't staying up nights dreaming of someday winning the Indy 500, but then again, I wasn't the average ten-year-old. While in some ways I was just like other girls my age, still playing with

Barbie dolls and baking cookies with my mom, I also spent most of my childhood watching my dad work on racecars, fascinated by his knowledge of engines and the technical engineering aspects of engines and body frames. I became equally intrigued by the sensation of driving fast—really fast. I come from a family of adventure seekers. The exhilaration I felt when I stepped on the pedal of my first go-kart was enough to hook me for life. I loved going fast and steering my kart around tight corners and barreling down the straightaways. I felt a freedom unlike anything I had experienced before that day. I got the same feeling as the one I get when I ride a roller coaster. Faster, faster. Woo hoo! At age ten, I had found my life's passion. From that point forward, I had a one-track mind. Instead of playing soccer after school or taking piano lessons, I dedicated myself to becoming the best race-car driver in the world.

Dreams lift us from the commonplace of life to better things.

—Henry Wadsworth Longfellow

In dream interpretation books, being chased by an animal or a shadowy creature usually represents one's passion or natural feelings. So I guess you might say that my childhood dreams were really projecting my future. Literally and figuratively, I now find myself being chased for a living. To be certain, it's far better to be chased than to be the one coming from behind, doing the catching up. My girlhood dreams of becoming a racecar driver are now my reality. I spent so many nights dreaming of what it would be like to win. In my mind I believed I won every race—and in my dreams I did. It's funny looking back, because in my dreams I often had to convince people that I had really won. I'd ask, "Did you see me? Did you see me win that race?" I always found myself trying to convince everyone in my dreams that I had won—that *I* was the winner.

My dreams weren't always about driving, but they were always about racing—whether I was running on foot in a race or using our driveway as a racetrack. Perhaps those dreams were an early foreshadowing of the years to come—of people doubting my skill, my drive, and my absolute ambition and determination. Why didn't anybody believe me? Why did they doubt my victorious outcome? Why did I continually have to prove myself?

Of course, I always recognized that these were just dreams—sometimes even nightmares—yet they were all vivid figments of my imagination. Or were they?

The truth is . . . they were more than just figments of my imagination. They became manifestations of my thoughts. There are no coincidences. My dreams projected the story of the following fourteen years of my life, to the present day and, I'm sure, well beyond the writing of this book. I no longer have those bad images, but my days of proving myself as a worthy competitor are far from over.

It takes twenty years to become an overnight success.

—Eddie Cantor

Phoenix, Arizona, 2006

The year 2005 was the most exciting of my fourteen years of driving. At twenty-three, I became the youngest woman to turn the world of IndyCar racing upside down, bringing the Series into the mainstream for the first time in many years. People often ask if I am surprised by the sudden fame and attention I've received this year? The answer is a simple "no." I'm not surprised at all. In fact, although I realize the amount of attention I've received as a rookie driver is out of balance with the norm, it is the last thing I thought about when it came to my career and my racing. There's a rare type of certainty that's hard to describe unless you possess it yourself. It's a level of self-confidence that straddles the line between secure and arrogant. It's a type of knowing—of self-belief that is unaffected by what others think or believe. Despite their opinions, it's the comfort to forge your own path. If you have it, you know what I'm talking about. If not, you probably know someone who does. It's that person who walks into a room and everyone wants to know who he or she is. It's a sense of confidence and self-assurance that one is born with—not the kind you develop through years of success or adulation. People say I've had that distinctive certainty my entire life. It's how I knew what my calling was at such an early age. It's like falling in love—you know when you know. You can't describe that feeling, but you know without a doubt it's the real deal.

Becoming a professional racecar driver is what I've worked for since the first day I sat behind the wheel of a go-kart in my hometown of Roscoe, Illinois. Mom and Dad took me and my younger sister on regular family outings to our local track. I loved the feeling of driving—of being in control, of using my head and outsmarting the other drivers. From day one, I knew *this* was my calling, my destiny, my dream—and I knew that someday I would it make my dream come true.

In 2005 the media introduced the term "Danica mania." I think people began to believe what I've always known—that I can compete, I can hold my own. I am equal competition—and yes, I can win. It was my rookie season as an Indy driver, and I shattered several IRL records, including tying for the most pole positions won by a rookie in the history of the sport and becoming the first woman driver to consistently qualify and place in the series.

Like any rookie, I've had to prove myself as both a driver and an athlete, qualifying more quickly and racing faster than my peers just to earn the respect that I deserved to be on the track—something I would otherwise have been given if I weren't seen as "the girl on the track" or as "driving the princess-mobile," to quote many of my critics (and some of the other drivers and their teams). You don't get to be an Indy driver without talent. Even the drivers who are at the back of the pack are skilled and capable drivers, but the back of the pack is the last place I want to be—ever, *on* and *off* the track. I like to win. I like to be number one.

I always had a need to be first. When I was a young girl, I used to race the boys back to the classroom from recess, just to see who could get there the fastest. (I usually won.) I wasn't one of those young girls who always (or ever) let the boys win in tetherball or four square. I was aggressive and had a will to win, even then. While my mother never told me to let the boys win, she did ask me to stop kicking them between their legs, something I did whenever I felt threatened or angry.

I was one of those girls who played just as rough whether I was competing against a boy or a girl. I never discriminated when it came to winning. In the seventh grade, I played basketball as a point guard on the junior high team. I was a pretty good player except for my hair, which always seemed to drape over my face during a game, making it hard to see the ball. I loved driving the basket, I played aggressively, usually fouling out at some point during the game, sometimes in the first quarter!

I play hard. I always have and always will. My dad was usually in the stands watching me with pride—especially when I fouled, thinking "that's my girl!" The other girls didn't understand my fierce competitive ways. I laughed at the referee. I called him names. I waved my hands in the air and questioned calls. You might say I sometimes went a little "John McEnroe" out there, but ultimately I wanted to win. My competitive spirit never allowed me to lay back and *let* anyone win. It still doesn't. I hope it never will.

My family, especially my dad, brought me up to believe that a game is never *just* a game. Playing anything against another person can be competitive. Backgammon, poker, basketball, golf, you name it . . . it's all got a competitive edge. Sometimes my basketball coach would tell me to chill out. He'd say, "It's just a game." But he was wrong. It was never *just* a game—at least not to me. What was the point of participating if I wasn't going to try to be the best? If I didn't give it my all? My dad taught me to never be satisfied with second place, and therefore I grew up believing you can always do better.

Even if I won, Dad showed me how I could have won by a bigger margin, gone a little faster, or improved on mistakes I made. (To be honest, he still does that!) That's the mind-set that was instilled in me at a very young age and it's pretty much how I move through the world today. I am one of those women who understands that when things get tough, it's time to push harder—to rise to the challenge, as opposed to caving in and surrendering. I will do whatever it takes to make something happen, especially when I want it so much I can taste it. That holds true in all areas of my life.

The word "impossible" simply doesn't exist in my vocabulary. If someone tells me I can't do something or will never make a successful attempt at something, I smell a challenge. I view their doubt as my opportunity to prove them wrong. I'll try harder than anyone else ever has just to make certain I can change the outcome in my favor.

Being told "no," "you can't," "it won't work"—I have to laugh just thinking about it, because every time I hear those words I have the same response: *Wanna make a bet?*

Even though I always had a high level of self-esteem and possessed the certainty I just spoke about, it hasn't always been easy for me to feel completely comfortable in my actions. I believe confidence and self doubt can coexist. The trick is to figure out how to be confident more often than not! You have to learn to doubt your doubt and to understand that fear is self-created and challenges can be met. Did I ever doubt myself? You bet. There have been so many times in my life and career when I wondered if I was strong enough, fast enough, pretty enough, good enough, and talented enough. There were times, especially in my teen years, where my confidence was so low I wondered if racing was just a fantasy. I was so down, and I had no support team— no one to talk to. My family was too far away, and I had no real friends nearby. It was incredibly lonely. I didn't have anyone I felt I could really rely on for support, both professionally and personally. But those years were really important in developing my inner strength and courage. They taught me that no one travels through life happy and confident all the time. How could you ever understand courage if you didn't experience fear? You can really feel loneliness only if you have also experienced unconditional love and support, something I grew up knowing from the inside out.

A lot of people have wondered why I am choosing to write a book so early in my career. To me, it doesn't feel too early. I have been racing and working for fourteen years! It hasn't been a cakewalk. No one handed me a thing. I earned my position in racing through lots of hard work, perseverance, determination, and dedication, and a lot of blood, sweat, and tears. If it were easy, everybody would be doing it, right?

Hard work always pays off. Achieving a high level of success is a difficult process, but it is so worth the chase. Success doesn't just happen. You have to go out there and make it happen. If you sit around waiting for success, it'll never come. In the end, all you'll be is someone just sitting around waiting for success.

With all of the attention I've received in the past few years, I think my story has inspired a lot of people. All different kinds of people — not just race fans. I'm a pretty ordinary girl who was blessed with extraordinary purpose and ambition. My story isn't one filled with a dark, jaded past. It's not one of overcoming addiction or battling some horrific disease. I'm not a young Hollywood starlet struggling with an eating disorder or partying my ass off night after night. I'm a small-town girl who had a dream and a family who helped her believe that anything is possible. I am living proof that if you work hard and aim high, you can do whatever you set your mind to, even if that makes you different. Take it from me. What makes you different makes you great. I know in my heart that being different is a good thing—it's certainly how I got here. I wanted to share my story so that anyone who has ever felt defeated or uncertain of her talents or her future can know in her gut that you have to pick yourself up, dust yourself off, and keep moving in a forward direction, no matter what obstacles lie ahead. This book is for all of us who have to navigate the daily speedway of life, who sometimes need a reminder to slow down or a push to get up and go, go, go. It's a book for all of you who were told "you can't," but you "did" anyway. I am proud of what I've accomplished and know the best is yet to come.

One the most rewarding aspects of all the attention I've received this past year is showing the world that women can do anything, but it's not just about a woman competing in a male-dominated sport. It's about being the best at whatever you do, regardless of gender. I didn't win the 2005 Indy 500, but I proved that a woman can compete at a top level in racing. For the first time in racing history, a woman placed in the top four and led for nineteen laps. For the first time in more than twenty years, an Indy driver made the cover of *Sports Illustrated*, and for the first time ever, that driver was a woman—and that woman . . . was me.

When you look in the side-view mirrors on your car, there's usually type at the bottom that reads "objects in mirror may appear closer than they are." If I had a mirror in my mind there might be a similar saying, except mine would swap the word "closer" for "bigger." I have big thoughts—sometimes bigger than they appear. I have never feared dreaming big or making the impossible possible. If you can think it, you can become it. I have known this since age ten. After I sat in my first go-kart, I never had a "Plan B." I was always going to be a professional racecar driver, whether that meant going to college to study engineering so I could learn how to build my own racecar or driving my dad's truck around my parents' office building to learn how to go faster even if I couldn't see over the steering wheel at the time! Whenever I wasn't on the track, it was always about racing. It was all I ever wanted to do.

Learning to exaggerate your mind means dreaming big and never giving up when you're defeated. A loss is still a learning experience. I spent my first season as an IRL driver in search of that inevitable yet elusive win. With every checkered flag and each fourth-place, tenth-place, or even eighteenth-place finish, I came off the track with more experience, more knowledge, and more drive than I had before the green flag was thrown. Every loss is an opportunity to learn and grow. I will never again have a rookie season in the IRL. With each step I took as a driver to get here, I set goals for myself, and one by one I have reached almost all of them along the way. If I ever stop dreaming big for myself, I know it will be time for me to retire.

My ability to see the next race as a win, or my next win as a step toward becoming the champion, is the difference between victory and defeat, regardless of the outcome of every race I run. One of my favorite sayings is "If you shoot for the stars and fall short, you'll still land on the moon." I'm not sure who taught me that, but it definitely guides my life. What would have been the point of reaching for Indy if I didn't believe I could win or positively impact the sport? If I never thought that what happened at Indy this year was possible, or if I never

Introduction

thought that I could be a part of bringing the IRL Series into the mainstream, I would have been completely unprepared for everything that happened this past year, let alone my entire life leading up to this moment. Instead of overwhelming me, the past fourteen years have been the most unbelievable and fantastic ride—one that I've enjoyed every minute, moment, and mile.

Chapter ONE

Learning to Drive

There are some things one can only achieve by a deliberate leap in the opposite direction.

—Franz Kafka

I saw my first go-kart when I was nine years old. A friend of my sister, Brooke, who lived in our neighborhood was into racing karts. I took one look and thought, "Ooohhh! This looks like fun!" My sister and I started off racing together, but she quickly lost interest. At the time, my parents had been thinking of buying a pontoon boat, but Brooke somehow convinced them to buy a couple of go-karts for us.

Even though I really wanted the boat, I accepted the kart because I didn't want to feel left out of all the fun.

Karting (go karts) is a type of open-wheel racing. In order for a kart to be legal for a race, it must have no suspension and no differential. Most kart tracks are relatively short, usually no longer than one half mile in circumference. Karting has become a very competitive sport for young drivers and is the best place for kids to start driving, especially those who have big dreams like me to go on to become professional racecar drivers. Karting continues to grow in popularity and has produced some of the biggest names in racing.

In the beginning, karting was a great way for our family to spend time together. When I began karting, all of my races were pretty close to Roscoe, Illinois, where I grew up. As my karting career progressed, we began to travel longer distances so I could compete in races at various tracks in Michigan, Ohio, Indiana, and Wisconsin. We spent endless hours (anywhere from one to twenty) in our family car on weekends traveling to and from races. At the time, we had a family truck with jump seats in the back. Dad usually drove, with Mom in the front. My sister and I were confined to the back. Later we expanded to a cab with a pop-up roof so we'd have more room. The cab had two temperatures—hot and cold, both of which made sleep uncomfortable.

Spending this kind of concentrated time with my family at such a young age taught me a lot of things, including patience, understanding, and sometimes the need for privacy! It also taught me the importance of keeping loved ones and those you trust close, something that would come in very handy as my career began to take off.

I grew up in a family in which my parents made it a priority to spend time with their kids. I also had parents who both had an interest in racing. My father, TJ, used to race snowmobiles, midget cars, and motocross bikes, starting in his late teens until just after I was born in 1982. Thanks to him, I grew up thinking about things most other ten-year-old girls aren't even aware of, such as RPMs, engine temperature, and how the other kids on the track might be working harder than I was. Dad's interest and knowledge of racing made my entrée possible. My dad's formula for success? To live, eat, sleep, drink, and breathe racing. It didn't take long before these thoughts became second nature to me—and I was officially hooked on driving karts.

Blessed are those who have not seen and yet believe.

—John 20:29

I started racing in the Junior Sportsman Stock class, which consisted of drivers from ages eight to twelve years and was made up of essentially all boys and me. The karts engines are 5 hp Briggs and Stratton, which most of you probably have in your lawn mower. I was a gawky kid who wore thick-rimmed glasses. I had long hair that itched my head under the weight of my helmet, not to mention the worst helmet head you ever saw. But I didn't care. I was having fun and loved what I was doing.

Six months into my first season, I was setting track records at the local karting track, Sugar River Raceway. Sugar River is a small track set in a wooded area, with trees all around, that flooded whenever there was a heavy rain. My first kart was black. I couldn't pick the color of my chassis, but I could pick the colors of my side pods and the color of my racing suit. My first suit was purple, with a big lime-green section at chest level that circled all around the front. D-A-N-I-C-A was written across the green chest section in large purple capital letters. There was no mistaking who the driver in the purple and lime-green suit was.

Soon after I began racing, I tasted my first victory on the track. I was in third place when the two drivers ahead of me crashed into each other and spun out, taking them both out of the race. I swerved around the crash, and with a couple of laps left, I sped my way to victory! I threw both my arms up in the air as I went across the finish line. I had won my first race! I had never felt such exhilaration. My heart was pounding so hard you could see it through my suit. I grabbed the checkered flag and proceeded to take my very first victory lap. I waved that flag with pride and pure joy. It felt awesome. I loved winning and I loved racing.

Every weekend I got a little faster, qualifying in better positions and improving my lap times. The weekend I won my first race I was a full 2 seconds faster than the next-best racer. My kart was perfect. It was fast, and from that race forward, I felt unstoppable. Although I had shown interest in other sports, including volleyball, cheerleading, basketball, and tumbling, I knew I really wanted to spend my time racing. Dreams of becoming a singer, an engineer, or a veterinarian fell to the wayside. Racing was my focus and my sole desire.

I've had the same goal I've had ever since I was a girl. I want to rule the world.

—Madonna

There are two entities that govern karting. The World Karting Association (WKA) is divided into nine districts and is primarily focused on East Coast racing. The International Karting Federation (IKF) primarily focuses on West Coast racing. I mostly raced WKA races. I raced in the Midwest, and our limited season was from April to late October. The racers on the West Coast could race year-round, so often they were better drivers because they had more experience and time behind the wheel. Local events lead to regional events, which ultimately lead to national events. In each race, you qualify by earning points, which are cumulative toward your championship standings. There are five regional races and five national races during the season. I usually raced in two regional series, for a total of ten races, and in one national series, for an additional five races. I tried to get in fifteen or more races during the year.

I spent my first season racing locally before I began traveling to other regions in the Midwest. By age eleven, I was shattering records everywhere I went, even setting two records in one day at Michiana Raceway Park, in Michigan. I wanted everyone to know that Danica Patrick was a force to be reckoned with and a name to remember. The press was beginning to write short stories, usually consisting of just a few sentences, mentioning me and the success I was having as a youngster in karting. My father called the editor of our local paper all the time to keep the momentum that was building.

Danica Patrick

My family sacrificed a lot to keep me on the track. Without their constant love and support I would never have been able to achieve my goal of turning professional. I learned at an early age that the success of a driver depends on the quality of the entire pit crew. Looking back on my early days of racing, my family was my team, my crew, my everything. Dad was literally my crew chief, engineer, coach, sponsor, and manager. My mother kept statistics. Brooke was also there to lend moral support and to root me on for every race. Brooke has a perpetual "glass half full" view of the world. She always sees the positive side of any situation. My family was the extent of my "pit crew." I did whatever it took to make them proud, to not let anyone down — especially myself.

My parents were middle-class working folks. They started their own business, a glass company, which was formed and first run from our family garage before growing into a much larger business that required office and warehouse space. Mom initially worked from the house, doing the accounting for the company in between changing diapers. The only college education between the two of them was the year and a half my mother spent studying accounting. My dad comes from the school of hard work and experience. He knows the value of working hard and understands how to push himself to do whatever it takes to get a job done (just in case you're wondering where I get these traits!). He is extremely driven and over the years built his business and became very successful.

As business grew for my parents, life became more comfortable around the house. We were able to afford my karting, which had become a very expensive weekend activity because of all the travel. My father always told me, "Speed costs money. How fast do you want to go?" My parents did whatever it took to see to it that I had all of the advantages in racing. To make sure I was able to attend races, my parents would sometimes drive through the night on Friday just to get me to the track early enough on Saturday, in the nick of time for the first race. Then we'd do it all over again Sunday night so we could be home for work and school bright and early Monday morning.

I loved following my passion. I loved that we followed this dream together as a family. I always had a sense of home with my family around. Brooke became as much of a best friend as she was a sister. It was much better being together than apart—something I would come to painfully understand a few years later when I was racing in England.

Even so, I knew there was no place on earth I'd rather be than on a track. I knew I was good at racing and it would be my job forever. I liked being different and wanted to do something the rest of my friends weren't. I was actually kicked off the cheerleading squad in tenth grade for missing too many practices and games. I didn't care too much. Cheerleading is fairly common for girls, and I did enjoy doing it, but it didn't set me apart like racing did. Driving allowed me a lot of opportunities I otherwise would never have experienced had I pursued another sport like softball, volleyball, basketball, track, band, or choir. I participated in all of these activities, but racing was my passion. It was exciting and different, and I loved it.

It didn't take long for me to understand that being the only girl driver made me different, and my presence on the track would not always be welcomed with open arms. Almost immediately, the boys were intimidated by my success. Somehow I understood that this would be an ongoing battle and issue throughout my career. I didn't care. I adored what I was doing and was determined not to be deterred by their lack of enthusiasm or the teasing that would follow as I became a leader in karting.

Looking back, I was probably a bigger bully than they were. In fact, I was really the one doing most of the intimidating at first. In one of my early races, I had developed a rivalry with another driver, Brian. Most of us were from southern Wisconsin, so we all knew each other and our families all watched our races together. During one race I decided I would let Brian know that I wasn't afraid of him. As we approached one of the last turns of the race, he came to the inside of me. The turn was a fast 90-degree corner. He approached, and I turned and drove right into the side of him, which knocked the chain off his kart, making him unable to finish the race.

My dad made me apologize after the race, but I didn't regret what I had done. We had a bona fide rivalry, and I decided to take a stance right there and then. He was a good racer, which meant he was my competition—and I was his. My father taught me to do whatever it takes to win as long as I was kind of fair and it was within the boundaries of the rules. He taught me to push the limits, so that I could break down barriers.

Rivalries are a part of all great sports. Racing is no exception. I still find myself battling rivals in every race I drive. Rivalries are what keep the sport interesting to the athletes and the fans. Yankees and Red Sox. Bobby Rahal and Mario Andretti, Michigan and Ohio State, Florida and Florida State—all great rivalries in sports history. All great games to watch, and better games to be playing in. I don't view a rivalry as a bad thing. I think it's a part of healthy competition. The better I got at driving, the bigger my rivalries grew, yet somehow, once the day was over and the races were done, because we were kids those rivalries were short-lived and were mostly played out on the track.

In between races the other kids and I would throw a football behind the trailers. I almost missed one race because I was so preoccupied with our football games. After the races, most of the families would go out for pizza together and reminisce about the day's events. It was a great way to spend time with my family. Race weekends were truly a family affair, and I look back on them with warmth in my heart and a fondness for days gone by when we all had the time to be together every weekend.

I'm often asked what it takes to become a professional racecar driver. Turning pro for a driver isn't like turning pro in basketball or baseball. The path for those athletes is pretty well mapped out. You play in school, maybe you play in college, and if you're good, you turn pro. For a driver, the path is slightly different. A young driver starting out has to have four things: a passion for the sport, the money to participate, confidence, and talent. I found my passion for driving early in life. Find what you're good at—do what you have a passion for. If you can make a living at it, you are among the luckiest people I know.

Unlike professional racecar drivers who have large corporate sponsors, go-kart drivers are pretty much sponsored by mom and dad, at least in the beginning. I was lucky that I grew up in a family that had the means to support my dream. My parents were not wealthy, but they were willing to give what they could so that I was able to explore my potential. Engines, clutches, carburetors, gears, new tires, side pods, helmets, suits, trailers, fuel, you name it . . . it's expensive.

My dad was brilliant when it came to building karts. He understood the mechanics and engineering of how to keep the engine running and ways to make the kart go faster. Because my dad used to race snowmobiles, midget cars, and motocross, he could build his machines from the ground up. He designed and created unique chassis and extra parts. His ability to inherently grasp what was needed to make my kart go faster was and still is remarkable. He just knew what to do. His knowledge and his application of information was a huge reason I excelled as a young racer. It remains a big part of my success today.

Confidence takes a racer a long way. Believing you are the best will help others see you as the best. There is no room for lack of confidence on the track. There are no "do-overs," no second chances, no second guesses. Split-second decisions are made—some are right, some are wrong. Having the confidence to make those decisions in the moment is the difference between a weekend racer and a professional driver, between winning and losing, and sometimes . . . between life and death.

Finally, a young racer needs talent. Without it, your season will inevitably end early with a crash or you will quit out of pure frustration from not performing well. Kids get bored so easily. You have to love racing or any sport you participate in to stick with it. There are a lot of kids out there who would love to be racing or participating in the sport you do. These are the same kids who are waiting for their opportunity to do what you're doing better than you. Be the best at whatever you do. Someone is always right behind you waiting to take your spot. That philosophy was drilled into my head by my parents. They cared if I didn't win, but they never judged me as long as I tried my hardest and gave a 100 percent effort. To them, 99 percent was unacceptable. If I didn't feel like going to practice, my parents reminded me that there were lots of other kids who would go in my place and would take the opportunities I had. For sure those kids would find a way to be at practice that day. There was no use in participating halfway, two-thirds, or even 99 percent. That was evident when I was kicked off the cheerleading squad. I enjoyed being a cheerleader, but I wasn't as committed to it as I was to karting. My racing schedule didn't allow me to be at all of the practices and games. I had to focus my attention on one activity or they would both suffer. It was a no-brainer. Racing. It was an all-or-nothing proposition in our home. That's the philosophy my parents instilled in me from the very start.

My First Crash

Driving a kart was fun. It came easily to me. I avoided getting into an accident for the first two years I karted. Some may say I was lucky—others may think I wasn't trying hard enough. My first crash happened at a national event in North Carolina when I was twelve years old. I was leading the race. It appeared that I was going to win. However, another racer had different plans for the outcome. As he entered turn one he didn't lift his foot off the throttle, and as a result I was punted and pushed off the track just after the start-finish line with one lap to go. He and another racer were able to pass me. I came around the track going into my last lap, now racing third. I was able to catch up with the two cars that had passed me as we approached the last corner. We all spread out. The driver who punted me was diagonally on my right. The other driver was farther over and directly to the right. We created a flying "V" as we entered the final turn. I was trying to stay left to pass if I could. As we entered the final turn, I never lifted my foot off the throttle and drove right over the top of the driver who had punted me. I drove over his left rear tire, which launched me over the top of him until I flipped my kart and landed right on top of him. My foot never left the floor. The victim of my lead foot was Sam Hornish Jr. (To this day, I still drive against Sam in the Indy Series.) Sam was as tough a driver at age twelve is he is today. I have respect for Sam. In racing you have to be tough, and Sam is definitely one tough driver.

My parents had never before witnessed me crash. This accident looked worse than it was. My dad came running out onto the track to see if I was OK. His feet couldn't quite keep up with his emotions. He tumbled, did a barrel roll, and without losing a step, got right back up and kept running toward me. He was there before the ambulance was on the track. Thankfully, no one was hurt. Sadly, I also lost the race. Despite my loss, I still had more racing to do that weekend. As I sat in my kart waiting to go out in another race, helmet on, my dad reminded me that I wasn't invincible. I thought to myself, "He's right." I never forgot those words.

At age twelve I moved up a series from Junior Sportsman, and began racing Juniors. The Juniors Series is for racers ages twelve to sixteen. After sixteen, the series is called Seniors. I continued my intimidation of the boys right up to starting Seniors. By age fifteen and sixteen, the boys I was competing against began to develop into young men. They were getting more aggressive, stronger, bigger, and more macho. That's also the age when boys start ignoring girls—especially the ones they like. It's their "boys are cool and girls are not" stage. Up to that point, I had struck a chord of fear in most of the other racers. I was small then, as I am now (most days!). Until the boys hit puberty and began to grow, they would see me coming and would turn the other way or say things like, "Oooo. There *she* is. Don't make her mad. She might beat you up." I loved it.

Granted, I had a temper. I felt no shame. If I got mad at someone, I let him have it. My father recently told me a story I had forgotten. He ran into a guy who works for Klein Tools, a company that is very involved in racing. They sponsor another team in the Indy Racing League. The gentleman told my father he had been berated by me when I was eleven years old. I was racing at Michiana Raceway Park in Michigan. During a practice run, I was cut off by an adult driver who was entering the track preparing for his practice session. As soon as he came into the pits I ran up to him, my voice trembling because I was so angry. I shook my finger in his face, saying, "Don't ever pull out in front of me again. Did you see what you did? Did you not see me coming? You need to look where you're going!" I went off on this guy. It's not that I didn't have respect for adults. I felt that he was being reckless—that he wasn't watching what he was doing. He jeopardized my safety on the track, and you have to respect the safety of the other drivers out there. Worst of all, I am sure he wrecked a good lap of mine!

Don't lose your temper; use it.

—Dolly Parton

I know that my temper has gotten in the way from time to time, but I also know that as racers, we all have a responsibility to be careful on the track. I don't care if I am perceived as being rude—or as a bitch.

Danica Patrick

Let's face it: As the only girl out there racing, I am "The Bitch" on the track whether I open my mouth or not!

I have never cared what anyone else thinks or says about me. I was only self-conscious about my skills as a racer and about my successes and failures on the track. I have never questioned my character, my personality, or my drive to be the best. That's unwavering. Call me names, doubt my ability. It has never stopped me from going out there and making a fool out of anyone who thinks I can't do it.

After a few races in the Seniors Series, I pretty much decided that go-karts were not my future—racecars were. I was becoming aggressive on the track—too aggressive to keep racing karts. My eagerness to move into Formula cars was beginning to get the best of me. My impatience was growing to move on to bigger challenges.

In my last karting race in Formula A, I was disqualified from the qualifying session for being one pound underweight. After qualifying, karts and drivers immediately go to a scale to be weighed in order to make the results legal and official. I battled my way through three heat races to give myself the best starting position possible for the feature event. After my nose cone folded under the front of my kart twice, it was impossible to drive. After stopping in the pits to fix it, I re-entered the track right in the middle of the leaders, but I was one lap down. The officials gave me a black flag, which means you are required to come off the track. I didn't listen. I kept going, and going and going, until I saw my mom standing on top of a hay bale waving her arms at me, signaling me to come in. Seeing my mom, I became aware I was doing something wrong. I came into the pits but didn't stop. I kept driving until I reached the garage, passing pedestrians left and right—a slight mistake on my part. A driver is never supposed to drive through pedestrian areas. A few weeks after that race, I was notified that my participation in the Series would not be accepted for the upcoming year. If I wanted to continue pursuing karting, this would have been horrible news. Thankfully, I had bigger plans: to become a professional car racer.

I wasn't sure if I would be accepted at the next level, but I was willing to do anything I could to find out. Since the early 1930s, women have competed in all areas of motorsports. One of the first was a British driver, Kay Petre, who competed in races driving her Wolseley Hornet. A woman racer was something of a phenomenon in those days—it kind of still is. Kay Petre was a small-framed, thin girl, standing just under five feet tall. She became an overnight superstar and a favorite of the media. Kay brought style and fashion to the otherwise usual racing image of dirty cars and dusty tracks. Hmmm . . . I know someone who fits this image too. By the 1950s women were driving in races called Powder Puff Derbys. These required very little skill, courage, or strength. The cars puttered along primarily for the enjoyment of the spectators—not for the thrill of the competition among the drivers. Of course, racing today is a lot more competitive and the drive to win is more important to the driver than it used to be, at least to this driver. I still have my sight set on someday driving Formula One, which I believe is the pinnacle of open-wheel racing. Formula One (F1) has had only a few women compete over the years and so far without great success. Maria Teresa Filippis and Giovanna Amati were among the first women to take a spin at the wheel of F One Racing in the early 1950s. Filippis has the highest recorded F1 finish for a woman, coming in tenth place against fellow racers, including Bernie Eccelstone, Carol Shelby, Phil Hill, and Sterling Moss. Years later,

Danica Patrick

Bernie Eccelstone admonished my participation in Formula Ford, making claims that women had no place racing, especially in Formula One. My father wrote him a letter after he made those disparaging statements, and we did receive a note of apology. And much to my surprise and delight, I received a Christmas present from him in 2005. In the end, I think he knows racing is about skill and speed—not what kind of body you have. It has also been my experience that someone speaks out against change when their existence feels threatened.

Women such as Lyn St. James, Janet Guthrie and Sarah Fisher, all of whom drove in the Indy 500 before I did, have each become synonymous with women in racing. These women broke down all sorts of barriers, which allowed at least one woman in the next generation of drivers to believe she could become a champion. Even at the age of twelve, I knew I wanted to be one of those drivers. I would continue to pursue my dream.

Chapter *TWO*

Trust Your Instincts

First thought, best thought.

—Jack Kerouac

eople ask me what it's like to drive a racecar? I explain that no two races are the same. In fact, no two laps around a track are ever the same, which means I have to be ready for anything and everything. I spend every moment in my car reacting to one thing and then the next. There's no way to pre-plan or go into a race with any kind of strategy because the circumstances can change so quickly. It's not like going into a business meeting, where you work from an outline, through bullet points, or follow an agenda. Racing requires an ability to get in that car day after day, trusting your skill, listening to and then following your instincts. You have to do your job regardless of the circumstances.

My first race as an IRL driver at the Toyota Indy 300 Homestead–Miami Speedway came to a crashing end—literally. Though I've crashed numerous times over the years, this was not how I wanted to go down in racing history for my inaugural IRL race. I was involved in a multi-car accident, which threw me into the turn-one wall. I'm told it was a spectacular crash that caught me in the middle of an eight-car pileup on lap 159. I say, "I'm told" because I don't remember very much about the incident. I know I was going underneath the crash as another car was slowly falling down the track until I clipped his wheels and—*pppfh!*—I ran straight into the wall. I've since reviewed the videotape of the crash and I saw myself crash, burn, and fall down the track until I came to a halt in the infield. I got out of the car, stumbled and swaggered like a drunken sailor, helmet still on my head, and literally tripped over myself as I tried to get to the medical van that had now made its way to me.

The next thing I remember is waking up and seeing a bright light. I had no idea where I was.

"Where am I?" I asked.

My mom was right above me, gently brushing my hair back from my face, saying, "It's OK, honey. You had a crash. You're in the medical center. You're all right; you're OK now."

"What's going on?" I asked. Over and over and over and over. On the way to the medical center, the nurse in the ambulance asked me if I realized I had asked her the same question several times? A little embarrassed, I decided to stop talking until we reached the medical center.

I had no idea whether I was seriously injured or had just suffered a concussion that was causing my amnesia and my repetitive questioning. I grew nervous when I realized I was in a curtained area of the medical center, with my family surrounding me and the track priest standing to my left. What was happening?

I was scared—petrified. I was afraid they were going to keep me overnight or send me to a mental institution. I was freaking out because I was acting so unpredictably. I was uncontrollably repeating myself and didn't know how to stop.

"Did it look bad?"

"Did the crash look bad?"

"How bad did it look?"

Now the medical center nurse was telling me I was asking her the same questions over and over again.

I had a severe concussion. To be safe, I was held for observation until later that night. I went back home to Phoenix to recover before I had to race again two weeks later. Thank God, the next race was in Phoenix. At least I wouldn't have to get on a plane, and I would have those extra few days to recover in the comfort of my own home.

I was pretty banged up. I spent the entire time between races sitting on my sofa with ice packs on my arms and hips. Little round pads stuck all over my body and around my muscles gave me electrical muscle stimulation, or micro-current, to help me heal faster. I also treated my concussion with light and sound therapy, using an earpiece to send buzzing sounds to stimulate my brain and softer, swooshing, calming sounds to help me relax. I wore goggles, which flashed light patterns that also stimulated my brain. It is a pretty progressive therapy that seemed to help my speedy recovery. It was not, however, a pretty look!

It's a scary thing to black out—to not have the ability to recall what happened a moment ago. But in driving, crashing is all in a day's work. You hope it's not part of every day's work, but it's always a possibility. My trust in my skill, my experience, and most important, being unshakable in my instincts is why I can get back in my car after a crash like the one I had at Homestead.

> **You have to trust your inner knowing. If you have a clear mind and an open heart, you won't have to search for direction. Direction will come to you.**
>
> **—*Phil Jackson***

Instincts and intuition are within all of us. I believe good instincts are mostly genetic. Though we all have the ability to sharpen or dull those traits, they are difficult to learn. My parents taught me at a very early age to trust my gut—to hear and then listen to that inner voice we all have. Dad taught me to think, listen, and learn—good advice that helped me strengthen my instincts. Learning to trust your instincts has a powerful impact on every aspect of life. Tapping into those feelings is the key to making split-second decisions and knowing, undoubtedly, that you are right.

Gut feelings exist for everyone. How many times have you found yourself saying something like "I just don't have a good feeling about this" or "Something's telling me this doesn't feel right?" Those are gut instincts. I know so many people who ignore those little messages and later find themselves regretting their decisions. As a racecar driver, I don't have time to question my gut instincts—my intuition that something's wrong or my instinct to make my move. One bad choice and the race is over. My career—and my life—depend on making split-second calls and trusting I've made the right decision in that moment. That trust and intuition are what allow me to do what I do. There's simply no room for "maybe" when you're moving at high rates of speed with twenty or more other drivers who are trying to win as much as you.

Have you ever been in a car accident? Needless to say, I have—several times—but my accidents are usually at speeds in excess of 200 mph, which means they happen so fast there's virtually no time to react other than by instinct. Racecar driving is a sport built on instincts. You either have good instincts on the track or you fail. Having good instincts is important, but it's not enough to survive as a driver. Trusting my instincts is what allows me to be on that track day in and day out, and what helps me to be a competitive force. Trusting my instincts also helps me greatly after hitting a wall or smashing into another driver at speeds that would frighten athletes twice my size. I know I can get back into my car the following week and not let flashbacks of a crash or a mistake I made negatively influence my next race. This is what I have been trained to do. In fact, those experiences just make me a better and more seasoned driver. I have an intuition that guides my decisions during every practice, every qualifying race, and every race day.

Danica Patrick

It was an interesting exercise for me to talk about specific races and to look back on my early experiences for this book. Everything on the track happens so quickly it's hard to remember the minute-by-minute details. It's very much like getting into an accident and not knowing exactly how it happened—it just seemed to happen so fast. Auto racing is a sport that is surely skill-based, but I believe it is equally instinct-based as well. That's why good drivers are always good drivers and reckless drivers will always drive recklessly. You can't teach yourself instincts. You can sharpen them, trust them, or deny them. Between talent and instincts, there's very little time for thought—only skill and good instincts matter. I know this seems like a lot going on at one time, but as a professional racecar driver, all of these traits become second nature. It comes from having instincts, gut reactions, and lots of time spent behind the wheel. When you start practicing a particular skill, any skill, at an early age like I did, and then continue to practice for fourteen years or more, anything you do consistently becomes inherent.

> **All of us do not have equal talent, but all of us should have an equal opportunity to develop our talents.**
>
> **—John F. Kennedy**

The physical demands of driving a car are very intense and can be rather extreme. It requires a tremendous amount of upper-body strength and endurance. When I am driving my car around a track for

200 laps, there's rarely a single moment when I can relax and glide. For the entire span of a race—sometimes two hours and as many as four—my muscles are working at maximum capacity without a break. On the larger oval tracks, muscle endurance is more important than strength because those races tend to be longer. I'm fighting the G-forces (the gravitational pull) in the same direction for every turn. On oval tracks, my car is designed to make only left turns. I literally fight the car to go straight. Road courses call for making both left and right turns, so the car is adjusted to essentially drive straight, requiring a lot more shifting and effort when making turns than on oval tracks. When I drive, I fight the gravitational pull, which makes my body weight multiply by that force. So, for example, if I am pulling 5 Gs during a turn, which is twice what a fighter pilot feels when he flies a jet, my normally 100-pound body feels like it weighs 500 pounds. That heavily factors into the strength it takes to hold onto my steering wheel to keep the car turning and on the track while moving at high rates of speed. The grip level of a track also determines how much strength it takes to drive my car. Racing on permanent circuits is harder than driving a street course, where oil and debris from everyday use are big factors that can cause the tires to slide.

All of my strength comes from the core or center of my body, from the hips up. The shorter the oval, the harder I have to work because I am turning sooner and the corners are tighter. There is not much time driving the straights of the track before I am turning left again and again and again.

I spend a lot of time training off the track, primarily running for endurance and doing yoga for a little strength but mostly for stretching. I find that holding my yoga moves during a workout session helps my muscles be in top shape and allows me to contract those muscles during a race for extended periods of time. While I enjoy yoga, I need to incorporate a hard-core weight-lifting routine into my training as well. My weight training is focused on strengthening my upper body, but I am careful not to unnecessarily bulk up in certain areas, like my biceps and triceps, since everything I do incorporates them anyway. My body responds very quickly to weight training, which means I can quickly add mass if I'm not careful. Adding mass is a good thing when I am driving road courses, which I do only a few times a year. I focus on my shoulders, back, chest, lats, and especially the scapular muscles, which are under the shoulder blades.

Cardiovascular training helps me control my breathing, which is extremely important because the faster I drive, more adrenaline rushes through my body and my breathing can become very exaggerated. Also, if I start to get tired driving, I find my breathing becomes heavier and I need to focus on the breath to stay steady. I run between forty and sixty minutes a day. Every day I'm not driving, I try to get in a run. It makes me feel happier and better about myself. When I don't get a run in, I feel a definite difference in my energy and confidence. I prefer to run outside if possible. If it's not possible because of weather or some other limiting factor, I prefer to use an elliptical machine over a treadmill. Using the elliptical also helps me strengthen my abs. I try not to hold onto the sides so I have to focus on pulling everything in tight and contracting my abdominal muscles.

I get so bored running on a treadmill. I feel like I am running in place. I'm an instant-gratification girl, so when I run outside I know I am going from point A to point B. Using the elliptical trainer is also easier on my hips than running on a treadmill, which is important to me since I've suffered several hip injuries over the years. The safety belts that strap me into my car are pulled very tight across my hips and chest. There are two belts in my groin area that loop at the end. Two belts come across each side of my hips, one with a latch and the other with a master lock that all of the straps lock into. The two shoulder harnesses come over the tops of my shoulders and latch into the master lock as well. The groin straps get pulled very tight and loop through the sides of the lap belts. The shoulder belts actually hold the groin straps in place, making it virtually impossible to move. Because of my size, the belts hit me right on my hip bones and lie on top of my stomach. If they were any lower, the straps would cut off the circulation in my legs. The straps feel like knives digging into my hips. There's no fatty tissue (OK, maybe a little) there to protect me, and they cannot put any padding there to protect me.

I used padding in the Toyota Atlantic Series, but in Indy, you race at higher speeds and the extra padding allows for more movement in a crash, which I don't want. I want to be held in my seat as tight as possible because it's safer. So that means I race in a constant state of excruciating pain and discomfort. As for the shoulder straps? Let's just say I'm waiting until I finish my driving career to get that boob job! (Now that's something you would never hear one of the guys say!)

After a race, the most important thing is to re-hydrate my body. I sweat profusely during a race, especially when the weather is hot. Even so, with my suit, the heat from the engine, and the effort I put forth, I burn thousands of calories of pure sweat. Although I try to drink enough water while I'm driving, it isn't always enough to keep me fully hydrated. There's a hole drilled into the front of my helmet where a pliable plastic tube is fed through, aimed directly at my mouth. This tube allows me to stay hydrated during a race. In order to take a drink, I have to pull down my balaclava (the head sock I wear under my helmet), feed the tube in, bite on it, and push a button on the back side of my steering wheel to get a drink. If the water is hot, and it often is since I race in warm climates, I have to pull the tube past my mouth and drop it down to my suit, push the button behind the wheel, and drain the hot water off the top, which wastes a lot of water. It can get so hot I can sometimes feel it burning against my chest. That is definitely not the water I want to take a sip of at 220 mph!

In many ways, racing is a lot like life—it's always changing. There are days when my car runs fast and others when it barely runs at all. Every other driver on the track has the same goal as I do—they're out there to win. They are out there sweating their asses off just like I am to do their best. The competition brings out good traits in all of us, yet sometimes I find myself dealing with a driver who makes a poor decision that impacts everyone else, especially when that idea turns into a dangerous situation. My physical health, my attitude going into a race, the conditions on the track, the weather, and the synchronicity of my pit crew all affect the result of the race, but at the end of the day, I am responsible for driving the car. Win or lose, I own the outcome. One of the most exciting and disappointing races of the season came with my final race of the season—the Toyota 400 at the California Speedway.

At the start of the season I told Danica I didn't care where she finished as long as she finished races this season. On-track success

**has certainly come quicker than I thought it
would, and she has done a magnificent job
balancing the demands in the racecar and the
demands on her outside of the car. It has been
a long journey for her to get to this point, but
in many ways the journey is just beginning. I
am very proud of what she has accomplished,
but I know the best is still yet to come.**

—Bobby Rahal

I am only a rookie once so this is the only time I can set rookie records.
Nobody puts more pressure on me out there than I put on myself. I
think a lot of people hoped that I would win at Fontana to bring a nice
ending to the season, but I looked at it as more of a beginning rather
than an ending. It was a season I will never forget. Coming into the
season I said I wanted to learn and improve. I also wanted to be
Rookie of the Year at Indy and for the IndyCar Series. I set those goals
and accomplished all of them. My year was successful regardless of
the outcome in Fontana. That said, a victory that weekend would
have really topped my year off nicely.

October 16, 2005, Fontana, California.
The Morning of My Last Race
of the 2005 IRL IndyCar Series Season

I qualified fourth for today's race—a position I am unsatisfied with.
It's the ninth time I qualified in the top five this season, and I am frus-

trated by my time, which was a "not quite fast enough" lap of 218.199. I missed my last chance to break the IRL IndyCar Series record for pole by a rookie, a record I currently share with Tomas Scheckter. The wind was a big factor in qualifying. Sometimes the wind works for a driver and sometimes against. On the track there is no way to predict the wind. And qualifying for a race is a lot different than driving in the actual race. A racer qualifies alone on a track. It's one car out there vying for the fastest lap time. Qualifying requires confidence and bravery in the cockpit to push your machine to go as fast as it can, reaching its very highest limit of cornering speed. Qualifying and racing both require a balancing act of driving skill, strategy, and teamwork.

This track is like many I raced during the 2005 season. I have been a good competitor for a rookie, and I expect to do well today. The race is a little longer than most, 400 miles, so I will have the luxury of time to work with the car in the 200 laps I'll make on this 2-mile oval before day's end. I have a chance to win today, but so do my teammates Buddy Rice and Vitor Meira. And Dario Franchitti, who grabbed the pole for today's race, edged out Tomas Scheckter and Sam Hornish Jr. They are all also strong competitors. The time difference between today's pole and my start in fourth position is barely more than 1 mile an hour. But in the world of auto racing, a single second is the difference between being first, fourth, and sometimes last.

I am fiercely competitive—I admit it. I am determined and focused like any top athlete with her eye on the prize. I like—no, make that *love*—to win. And as a barely 5'1" woman, I have to work a little harder to pull that off. It's not easy work piloting an 1800-pound rocket ship at speeds sometimes as high as 240 mph—especially when I weigh in at less than most seventh-grade boys. Think of it this way: Takeoff speed for a small jet airplane is 110 mph, and a 767 jumbo jet takes off at 175 mph. That ought to put a little perspective on how fast I drive!

Some critics have said that my weight is an advantage, that perhaps the car goes faster because I am lighter than the other drivers. What I lack in weight I have to make up for in strength. Today's race will require a tremendous amount of upper-body strength because it is one of the longer races. I've been told that I don't look as strong as I am, but anyone who has ever shaken my hand realizes there's a lot of strength in this tiny frame. In fact, my handshake gets a lot of buzz in the media. My father taught me to have a strong handshake and to look people in the eyes when you meet them. He said, "Shake it like you mean it!"

> **Don't be fooled by the pink nail polish. Danica takes your hand and it's like a truck driver. That's the yin and yang of Danica. The exterior is nice and pretty—and underneath she's as tough as steel.**
>
> **—Bobby Rahal**

There's a fine balance between being strong and looking too muscular or masculine. My husband, Paul, a renowned physical therapist for elite athletes, helps me train to keep lean muscles and avoid bulking up while strength-training. Mark Mulder, a friend and a pitcher for the St. Louis Cardinals, was working with my husband last year to strengthen his shoulders. One of his exercises was to lie on his side, with his left elbow on the ground in a plank position and his right arm across his stomach. He was supposed to lift a 5-pound dumbbell straight up to strengthen his pitching arm and shoulder. At the height of my 2005 racing season, I was using a 12-pound weight for the same exercise—twice as much as this professional ballplayer. Racecar drivers are freaky strong. We have to be.

I am not one for excuses. If my car goes faster, it's not because of my weight or size. It's because I have a faster car and I am a better driver than the others on the track. This is my job, my chosen profession, my passion. I work hard and expect only the best outcome every time I get behind the wheel. I take it hard when I don't win, but I try not to beat myself up. I race every race the same. I try my hardest, and I go out there to win. Sometimes things go wrong that are not in my control, like mechanical problems or crashes. There's not a lot I can do about those kinds of losses. But when I make a mistake, like stalling the car in the pits or turning my ignition off during a race, I have to take responsibility for those errors. Those days are the toughest. Every loss is one step closer to a victory. No two races are alike, which means I am learning something new every day I drive. I totally recognize I'm one of those fortunate people who go to work every day and do what I love. I drive—fast. I compete and, to be certain, I am out there to win.

It's twenty minutes before the race is scheduled to begin. There's been some discussion of moving the start time up because of the unexpected early morning rain. The California Speedway is a large oval track. It's big, it's fast, and when it's wet it's more than dangerous. It can be deadly. Greg Moore, a rising star on the IRL, was killed in a crash during his race at Fontana on October 31, 1999, at the age of twenty-four. There's no room for error today. I know everyone is here to see me do one of two things: win—or crash. Let's hope it's the former. I've had a tremendous rookie season, but I've yet to see the checkered flag come down on my car first. It takes an average of thirty-three races for most rookies to score their first win—Fontana is my seventeenth IRL race, and the last race of my rookie season. I am determined to do it today, and if not today, I will beat the average because by now you know there's nothing average about my drive to win.

I suit up and mentally begin to prepare myself for the race. As has been the case for every race this season, my husband, Paul, is by my side. He is an incredible stabilizing energy in my otherwise frenetic world. When I'm moving at my usual pace of 220 mph, both on and off the track, Paul balances things with his calm and even manner. He understands my competitive nature and my intense focus—especially on race day. He knows when to give me space and when I need his arms around me for comfort and support. He truly is the yin to my yang.

It's almost time to go. Dad leans over the wall (which divides pit row from the technical area my pit crew maintains during the race), gives me a hug and a kiss, wishes me good luck, and tells me to "have fun" before I go, something he has done since my first go-kart race.

Paul does the same. The moment has come for me to shut out the distractions and focus only on the task at hand. In one fluid motion, I'm sitting in my car, my crew strapping me in as I put on my gloves. With 50,000 fans still getting settled in the speedway stands, I know it's time to put on my track face, though I've worn this look of determination for hours leading up to this moment. I can't hear a sound beyond the beating of my heart, which pounds a little faster now against my suit. I can also hear my engineer, Ray Leto, in my headset, systematically going over today's final strategy. Paul and my parents also wear headsets, which are directly connected to all communication between me, my engineer, and my spotter. It's a real insider's perspective to listen to a race from the driver's seat.

All races involve a lot of communication between the driver and the crew. I don't pick my crew and they don't pick me. As a driver, I'm ultimately hired by a team owner. The crew is hired by the COO of the team. We all trust that we're there because each of us is the best person for the job. This trust is what creates strength, energy, optimism, and that "X" factor for a team. You can't buy true trust. It's essential.

A good example of this is the relationship I have with my spotter. My peripheral vision is limited to what's directly in front of me. I cannot see a car directly to my left or right. Anything visible behind my hands on the steering wheel is out of my line of sight. I heavily rely on my engineer and spotter to help me on the track. They tell me when I can make a move to pass, when I should drop back, when I should come into the pit, and when there are cars making moves on me from behind or beside me. Without them, I'm driving blind.

The Cardinals turned me down at age eight.

My sixth birthday! Brooke, Dad, and me ready to eat my Jem the Rocker cake.

Bev Patrick

I remember the outfit to this day. Glad I forgot about the hair.

Yes, I was a cheerleader. This was before I was kicked off the squad.
Hononegah High School

My younger years

If you can't beat 'em, drive over them! Sam Hornish, Jr. and I collide at Charlotte, North Carolina.

T.J. Patrick

T.J. Patrick

Speed Graphics 1994

Dousman, Wisconsin. Learning to drive.

A rare smile in England with my rare blond highlights.
Sutton

Racing Formula Vauxhall in England, 1999.

Second in the 2000 Formula Ford Festival.
A happy day in England.

At home during my recovery from Homestead.

OK, so sometimes I look
like my dad.

Walking away from a blown
engine at Cleveland, Ohio.
Mom's always by my side.

Concentration and
competition.

Tough day. *Paul Webb*

Tommy Kendall trailing me
in Long Beach just as he will
do after the race—on a leash.

Paul Webb

Paul Webb

Racing in the Barber Dodge
Pro Series, 2002.

Paul Webb

Bob Rahal congratulating me
on my first podium at my first
race in the Toyota Atlantic,
Monterey, Mexico.

Checking my makeup.

Paul Webb

Paul Webb

Does this smoke make
my butt look big?

Fresh tires are just
like a new pair of
shoes—they feel so
comfy when you
first put them on!
Brian Spurlock

Before my first appearance on *The Late Show with David Letterman*.

A picture is worth a thousand words . . . or more.

George Holz/Contour Photos

"Drivers, start your engines!"

The opening announcement at every race used to be "Gentlemen, start your engines." Not anymore . . . not while I'm around anyway. Yeah! I'd be lying if I said I didn't think that was really cool! Regardless of how a race is announced, I get the same butterfly feeling in my stomach, especially sitting on the track in virtual, almost surreal silence waiting for those four magical words. But it's a momentary feeling because when I hear the rumble of my engine, the symphony of all the engines on the track, butterflies turn into dragons. I know I have a job to do and today is my last chance this season to bring home that elusive "I want it so much I can taste it" win.

For the fans, this race was an exciting one to watch, with seventeen lead changes among seven drivers—me included. All day I had jockeyed my way from the back of the pack to eighth place, sixth place, and then first. I'm not sure whether the energy on the track was elevated because it was the last race of the season, there was some political agenda being played out, or I was being sent some sort of message that Danica mania was coming to an end. All day I felt that some of the drivers were trying to tell me to go home. The track is no place for a woman. They had perhaps had it with all of the media and other attention I received this year. Perhaps it was my own perception. Who knows? With twenty-five laps to go, I fought my way from being pushed into the infield grass by Jaques Lazier, driving a pink car for Team Target. I thought to myself, "Who's driving the "princess-mobile" now, huh?"

Danica Patrick

I radioed a message to my crew that he was driving like a jackass. He was making me uncomfortable with his reckless and erratic driving. We were battling each other for eighth place with just fifteen laps to go, at a speed of 212 mph, when Lazier drifted 6 feet—the equivalent of a football field in racing—and smacked into the back right side of my car. His bump sent both of us into a high-speed spin on the banking of the oval in turn four. The sound can only be described as a muffled, low-pitch explosion with crunching, crackling, and breaking noises as the bodywork breaks, creating debris that scatters everywhere after the car hits the wall. As you slide down the track, there is virtual silence. My focus turned to the oncoming cars heading right for me at 200-plus mph. Though I couldn't see the flames, they were shooting out from under the car as I spun too many times to count, finally hitting the wall in what felt like a hard crash before coming to a stop. We were both done with the race. I had been complaining to my engineer about Lazier's driving all day. I felt like I spent too many laps of this race going around in this vicious circle with his pink car. His irresponsible and thoughtless driving ended my rookie season with a crash instead of my much-hoped-for victory. I was furious.

Do you want to know what it feels like to get hit by another car during a race? Think of it this way: Have you ever been in a parking lot when a shopping cart dings your car? Does that make you mad? Have you ever been in a minor fender bender that wasn't your fault, going, say 20 mph? Did you get out of your car and lambaste the other driver? Multiply that feeling by 1000 and you might begin to understand why a racer gets mad when he or she is taken out of a race by the carelessness of another driver. We all go out there with the same goal. As professionals, none of us goes out on the track intending to crash, but we all know it's part of the job. It's an aggressive and competitive sport. It's high-speed poker. It's the ultimate game of slap. If you pull your hands away in time, you're safe. If not, you'll get hit—and hit hard. But racing, like all sports, is political. There are rivalries among drivers. We push each other's buttons out there. It's part of the play. Learning other drivers' characteristics and habits—how rough they drive or their intimidation tactics, whether they'll move over for you, where they like to drive, whether they like to drive on the inside or outside groove—it's all part of the learning experience and is a guessing game until you have the chance to race side by side with each and every one of them. Once you learn the characteristics of those drivers, it becomes part of your strategy in knowing how to pass them and what to expect from them.

Like any high-stakes event, there's a lot of emotion on the track, especially when there's a battle for place. But I didn't deserve to end my season this way. No . . . not *this* way.

Thankfully, as hard as I hit the wall, and despite the potentially life-threatening flames that shot out from my car during my spin, I wasn't hurt, and even if I was, I was too angry to notice. I could hear my engineer in my headset telling me to stay in the car until help came, reassuring me that the car was not on fire. I was too incensed to stay still. I got out of my car, looking for Lazier.

The race officials insisted I go by ambulance to be checked for internal injuries. I'm not sure whose idea it was to put Lazier and me in the same ambulance, but I am glad they did. I had a few choice words for Lazier, and like it or not, he was my captive audience. Although I had a badly bruised elbow, I managed to get close enough to him during the short ride to let him have it. I didn't hold back in telling him how I felt about his driving. Let's just say it wasn't my most ladylike moment of the season, and my mom told me to "always be a lady." It didn't take long for the rumors to start. One race official later told my parents that before he left the pit area, he had heard that I had open-hand-slapped Lazier. By the time he got to the garage area, he had heard that I closed-fist-punched him. Finally, by the time he got to our team hospitality tent, he had heard that I beat the crap out of him.

It turns out that Lazier himself was actually telling people I punched him, even admitting it to a newspaper the next day. To be honest, I wish I had. But the truth is that I didn't. I did give him a nice shove to the head to let him know I was unhappy—*really* unhappy. I find it funny that he lied about being beat up by a girl. That's not something most racers would want their peers to know! Now that the dust has settled, although I did not actually slap or punch him, I can now admit that I did give his head a little help meeting the van door.

Chapter THREE

Strength in the Pits

Don't look back. Something might be gaining on you.

—Leroy "Satchel" Paige

As a racecar driver, I rely on many different people in doing my job. The outcome of each race is dependent on every member of my team working in sync. If my car is not running right for a race, my engineer and mechanics have failed to do their job. If I lose time in the pit, my pit crew has dropped the ball. If I stall in the pit or make a damaging move on the track, then I am responsible for the loss. Every practice, every qualifying, every race is dependent on each element of the team being on their "A" game that day. I have to trust that my team is fast and that my engine is fast, and that collectively the team and I share the trust and confidence to bring home the win.

While my job is dependent on the quality and performance of my team, my team off the track is equally important. I'm so blessed to have parents who support all of my endeavors. My parents are an important part of my racing and now a huge part in building Danica Racing, Inc., literally running the business of my racing and career off the track. Together, they are there to support me whether I win or lose. They're around for the good, the bad, and sometimes the ugly. They're there when I didn't do well during a practice or a race, and they are there to celebrate a victory, whether it's the fastest lap time that day or winning a race. They cheer me up when I need it and can be ruthlessly honest, whether I want to hear their words or not. They're protective and removed at the same time. They know when I need something, and they understand my need to be alone (another trait I inherited from my dad).

> **The parents of prodigies convey enthusiasm without conveying expectation. They reward their children for trying as much as winning.**
> **—Emily Greenspan**

When it comes to my racing, my father has to be off by himself, away from the crowds. He is extremely passionate, to the point of almost being misunderstood. To watch him, an outsider might misconstrue his behavior as being a little over the top or aggressive. He shouts, stomps his feet, pounds his fists, and slaps his hands to his head, in a combination of frustration and nervous exhilaration. He's frustrated by mistakes I sometimes make or errors that happen in the pit. He is utterly exuberant witnessing his daughter live out her dream. How lucky am I to have a father who is so supportive and into what his daughter is doing? I'm so grateful, and I count my blessings every day.

His intuitive and brilliant insight into the second-by-second strategy of each race is keenly if not astoundingly accurate. I'm his kid out there on the track. He just wants me to have every advantage possible so that I can succeed. He's no different than a lot of dads who watch their children compete and excel. Some parents go to their kid's soccer games, while others coach the team. My dad was never a stand-on-the-sidelines type of parent. He has been my greatest coach because he's my life coach both on and off the track.

Dad is my touchstone. He's my honest guy. Dad tells it like it is, whether I want to hear it or not. He has a no-nonsense approach to life, and he has taught me that tough times make tough people. When I was younger, it really bothered me that he lacked any kind of filtering when it came to what he thought and how he felt. Sometimes it hurt my feelings. What little girl wants her father to tell her she sucks or she screwed it up (whatever "it" is)? Dad taught me to not ask the questions if you don't want to hear the answers. Boy, has that been a tough lesson.

Maybe I was young and immature, but there were a lot of years when I simply wasn't up for the critique. Dad speaks his mind without hesitation or consideration of my sensitivity, so sometimes it was hard to hear what he had to say. I know I seem all hard and tough on the outside, but sometimes it was really hard to hear what he had to say because the harsh reality was he was telling me the truth, warts and all. It's what I live and drive for.

I constantly asked questions, somehow expecting Dad to be softer, kinder, and less blunt. Nope. Not my dad. He consistently gave me honest answers—some that I didn't like and some that made me feel pretty good. Dad told me when I screwed up. He gave me each detail of how my performance could have been stronger, faster, better. He never missed an opportunity to point out ways to improve my driving. But he also told me when I did well, when I made him proud. He loved basking in the moment of kicking someone's ass out on the track, as if he had done the ass-kicking himself. Nothing beats seeing my dad beam with pride and joy after a race. It's the best feeling in the world.

Mom is the polar opposite of Dad when it comes to watching a race. Whenever I'm on the track, she stands in the pit—intense, quiet, and focused. She watches the race on a monitor that allows her to see how fast I'm going, what lap I'm on, and what's happening technically with my car from an engineering perspective. Mom is the definition of cool, calm, and collected, unless you notice her hands, which are tightly clenched together, her knuckles constantly grasped in the cup of her other hand for the entirety of every race. I know watching my races is nerve-wracking for her. But she trusts me more than she trusts any of the other drivers, so she places her faith in me to go out there and do my job.

As I was growing up, Mom referred to herself as the "referee" of the household. She kept the peace between Brooke and me, Dad and me, and anyone else who fought! She's quiet, but she's ever aware.

Nothing gets by Mom. She's funny, quick-witted, and extremely sharp. Having her trackside during a race means the world to me. She is the calming factor in what is otherwise a crazy environment. She walks the grid with me, stands with me when I'm putting my helmet on, and stays with me until the grand flag.

A mother understands what a child does not say.

—Anonymous

Simply knowing she's there is very comforting. Having her there when I need her is incredibly reassuring. I like having her by my side to console me if I need it, to laugh with me when something is funny, and even to poke a little fun together. My strong need for her presence increased during the three years I spent alone in England. Before I went to Europe, I didn't know what lonely felt like. I had always had my family around. Knowing my parents are there for me, supporting me and cheering me on feels so good, so full, so complete.

My mom has fallen into the role of "honorary mom" on the road. Some members of my crew come to her from time to time asking for advice that only a mother can give. She spends more time standing with the pit crew than I ever have. So they've developed their own rapport. If you ask my mom her opinion, just like Dad she'll give you an honest answer, but hers comes in a gentle manner.

Mom has imparted some good motherly advice over the years, but the one thing she is insistent about is that I always be a lady. I went through a phase when I decided that I'd swear a lot. She detested the way I sounded. She was right, just like she was right when she told me to stop beating up the boys and kicking them in the balls. She protected me from making a fool of myself and looking silly. There have been plenty of times in my life, especially after a race, when I have to remind myself to be a lady. Fontana was one of them.

Having my parents present at the track helps me stay focused on every level, but on race day they are a key element in the recipe that determines the outcome of my race. The first time I raced a go-kart, my dad told me to "just go out there and have fun." He started every go-kart race telling me that. To this day he still says, "Good luck, and have fun."

> **Once you say you're going to settle for second, that's what happens to you in life.**
> **—John F. Kennedy**

My family offers me a type of unconditional support that's hugely important to me on and off the track. I feel protected by my family and their presence at the track, but lately even more so. Things can sometimes get a little out of control, and they especially did during the height of Danica mania in the 2005 season. Autograph sessions sometimes turned ugly, with crowds getting so big that people pushed and shoved one another just to get to me. It's a part of my fame I simply don't understand. I will sit and sign autographs until the last fan leaves, but aggressive action to get to me is funny. I think, *"Who am I?"*

I know my parents will take care of friends and business associates who come to a race, making sure their experience is as enjoyable as possible. I want my guests to feel the excitement of being at a race, to feel the same rush of adrenaline I feel at the beginning of a race, to share the experience and understand why I chose to miss my senior prom and homecoming dance and to be on the track each and every weekend. My childhood friends are still my closest friends. They supported me year in and year out. Having them cheer me on helped me get to where I am today. Even though I don't have as much time as I would like to see them more regularly, they know how important they are to me, and hopefully they know how much I've appreciated their support throughout the years.

Danica Racing has also become a big business. I never dreamed I'd be the CEO of an entity with my name on the door. I always had my focus on driving. Because of that, I have placed my trust in a team of business professionals who, like my driving crew, must be on their "A" game each and every day too.

For me, whether it's the Rahal Letterman team, my Danica Racing team, or my friends and family who make up my support team, it all boils down to trust. There were times in my racing career when I had placed my full trust in other people to manage and bolster my career and was disappointed by their efforts. There were a lot of promises made along the way that were not delivered. It is always better to under-promise and over-deliver than it is to say you'll do things and not keep your word. It has taken me years of mistakes to understand that a great portion of my success relies on placing trust in my team. It's crucial to be particular when it comes to the people you surround yourself with. I am so lucky that everyone—my husband, my parents, my lawyer, my agent, my racing team, my teammates, and my friends—are all people I know I can unconditionally trust. It wasn't always that way. Once you lose someone's trust, it's very hard to earn it back. That's a lesson I needed to learn only once.

I spent three years, from age sixteen to nineteen, racing in England. Upon my arrival, I placed unconditional trust in the team, the mechanics, the engineer, and my managers who sponsored my trip abroad. I fully believed they had my best interests at heart. I don't think it was intentional on anyone's part, but I never received the kind of attention, equipment, or guidance I expected. Every time I asked for a better car, I was told I'd get one, but I never did. I asked for help from my manager, and he promised to defend my needs to the team, but things never changed. After my first year in England, it became painfully obvious that I couldn't trust what anyone was telling me as far as racing was concerned. As a driver, the strength of your team dictates everything. They had lost my trust, and to be honest, I don't think they cared because there was never a real effort made to earn it back after my first year there. I felt like they gave up on me before I ever had the chance or equipment to prove my grit. Conversely, I totally believe in my team now. In the deepest part of my heart and soul I know without question that my team at Rahal Letterman Racing believes in me. It's an incredible feeling to have that in my life because prior to signing my deal with Bob Rahal, I never had that kind of support. Each person around me gives me perspective, guidance, and insight in areas where I simply have no knowledge.

My parents have been married for more than twenty-five years. They have gone through every type of road bump I might experience with Paul in our marriage. Their experiences help shed light on how

I want to handle my own marriage. My parents have led both their children by example. Though Paul and I aren't exactly the same people as my mom and dad, I think our relationships are parallel on many levels. Like my dad, I have a temper, whereas like my mom, Paul is non-confrontational. It's a good balance, and seeing my parents successfully make their marriage work, even through tough times, shows me the importance of commitment and communication in my own marriage.

On the track, I couldn't ask for a better team than the one I have in Rahal Letterman Racing. Bob Rahal has had my best interests at heart from the very beginning. He wants me to be successful and has offered me the very best chance he can to win races. Every time I see Dave, he tells me how proud he is. It makes me feel really good to have his support and confidence. One thing for sure is that he is extremely proud of all his drivers and the team.

David Letterman grew up in Indianapolis. The "Dave" people see on television is different than the "Dave" I see at the track. David Letterman is serious about racing. That passion began when he was a child watching many of the legends at the "Brickyard." He grew up near the Speedway, where he saw his first race at age eight. He was dazzled with the speed of the cars and the skill of the drivers. He is far from a casual observer. Dave is very knowledgeable. The first time I went to his office I remember being totally blown away by all of the books there. He has books everywhere on every imaginable subject. I enjoy reading, but clearly not as much as he does!

It's an expensive proposition keeping a driver in a racecar. It can cost upward of $8 million a season for the team owner to keep a single driver on the track. Bob and Dave believe in me enough to see to it that every member of my crew is the best in the business. Bob, Dave, and Scott Roembke, the COO of Rahal Letterman Racing, are the driving forces behind our incredible sixty-five-member team. Scott is responsible for all facets of the team's operation, overseeing the coordination of the race operations for the team while managing its business and marketing side off the track. Steve Dickson and Bill van de Sandt are two other executives from Rahal Letterman who help me do the very best job I can. Steve is our team manager for the IndyCar Series, acting as a liaison between the IRL and our team. Bill is our team coordinator, handling the increasingly difficult job of coordinating the logistics for our three-car team. Jim Prescott spent two seasons as my team manager during my Toyota Atlantic Series racing. He oversaw my development as a driver in that series and helped me make my jump to racing in the IRL. He was an integral part of Bob Rahal's Rookie of the Year season in 1982, and he certainly added to my following in his footsteps as Rookie of the Year in 2005.

I am blessed to have one of racing's most experienced engineers in open-wheel racing as my technical director and lead engineer. Ray Leto is a perfect match for a driver like me. He is my calm, warm breeze when I feel a hurricane brewing. When I am behind the wheel, it is Ray who is guiding me the most on the track. He and I are in constant communication. The sound and tone of his voice is soothing to me as he is very steady, positive, and methodical, and helps keep me balanced throughout a race. He monitors every aspect of what is happening on the track, from other drivers to track conditions to the performance of my car. He is the person who briefs me going into a race and who tells me how I can be stronger next time around.

Ed Daood is my crew chief and chief mechanic. He's the guy who keeps the #16 Argent Mortgage/Honda/Panoz/Firestone car running in tip-top shape. (Hey . . . I got those sponsors in!) Ed has been the crew chief for drivers including Alex Tagliani, Adrian Fernandez, and Andre Ribeiro when they all won their first Championship Auto Racing Teams (CART) races. His invaluable experience with young drivers was a big asset in my 2005 rookie season and will continue to be a major contributing influence in upcoming seasons.

With a team composed of such experts in their respective fields, it's no wonder I had such a record-setting year in 2005. I trust this team of professionals with my life—literally. They know what they're doing. Who am I to say what to do as a rookie when these men collectively have decades of experience? I certainly bring my own ideas and input when it comes to the car. They listen to what I have to say, but I never question these experts or their experience. We trust each other and listen to our instincts. I feel, I listen, and I communicate what I think is happening. If my team didn't weigh in and take into consideration my experience driving, it would be like going to the doctor knowing something isn't quite right and the doctor telling me to go home, insisting I am fine.

All in a Day's Work

When I get to the track for a race week, I rely on my team's information as much as they rely on mine. Through the advent of computer technology, my team has access to discs of information containing everything from speed traces, to RPMs, steering lateral Gs, and breaking traces. Some drivers review their discs like football players looking at scrimmages or past games. I am simply not that kind of driver. I always tell Ray not to give me the discs because, truthfully, I won't look at them. I'm not a data geek. I'll work hard when I'm at the track, but I'm not studying my races the day after, because I don't get anything more from it.

A race week is composed of arriving at a venue several days prior to race day. For me, those days are usually made up of attending drivers' meetings, attending press conferences, practicing, and qualifying, which all builds up toward the culmination of the week's work: race day. Drivers' meetings are mandatory for all racers. It introduces the drivers to the track, which is especially important if you've never driven the venue. It's also an opportunity for drivers to ask questions about the upcoming week and to get clarity on commitments and expectations. The drivers receive track maps, which show us where the different facilities are located, such as the medical station and stations for our corner workers, who monitor where it's safe to pull off the track during practice or the race. Drivers' meetings are primarily about organizational aspects for the week and various procedures and protocol under possible scenarios that can occur during a race, such as a yellow flag, where we might be instructed to come off the track at turn four or to drop below the white line in the back straight if we plan to pit. Every track has a slightly different setup, so it's important for the drivers to attend these meetings. Even if they're a little boring, the information we get impacts race day. We also have to attend another meeting on the morning of race day in which we're updated on the same procedures.

I can't speak for every driver, but I have certain superstitions or rituals that I follow every time I get into my car. It might involve wearing the same T-shirt if I've had an especially good practice wearing that shirt. I always get into my car from the left side. I try not to get too caught up in the rituals because I can't let my day revolve around things I'm "superstitious" about, but I am aware of my lucky charms, and I use them, especially on important days.

Before I climb into my car I have a mental checklist of items I need before I put my helmet on. Ear plugs? Check. Gloves? Check. Balaclava? Check. Helmet? Check. Once I climb into the car I try to calm my mind as I am strapped in. I have a headset and microphone built into my helmet, which allows me to communicate with my team while driving. There are a handful of people not associated with my crew who wear headsets that are programmed into the same channel as mine. Many people, including my team, my parents, my husband, and special guests to the track that day, and anyone in the stands who has a headset can tune into my channel and hear what I hear and say throughout the race. Mostly they hear my spotter calling, "Inside, outside," which tells me where cars are above and below me on the track. The other person I communicate with on the headset is my engineer, who gives me information about pit strategy, and I continuously inform him about how my car feels throughout the race.

Waiting for the green flag, I feel as if my mind goes numb. It's hard to explain, but as I jump into the moment of it all, I have to clear my head of any outside thoughts that might distract my focus and attention away from the task at hand. I look through my shield and sometimes think, "There's my mom" or "There's Paul," but I am not wondering if I left the coffee maker on or if I ordered the invitations for my wedding! When I'm in the cockpit, it's all business. It's my job, and there's no room for mistakes. Anything that might distract my attention simply takes a backseat while I'm driving.

Danica Patrick

Practice sessions are really important to drivers, especially some-one like myself who wants as much time on the track as possible be-fore a race. Practice sessions are my preparation for qualifying. I am as focused for a practice as I am on race day. In fact, if I've never been on that particular track before, as was the case for sixteen of my seventeen races in 2005, I get a little nervous before my first run. To be honest, I get nervous every time I get in my car before my first lap. Who am I kidding? It is so crucial for me to do well every time I'm on the track, I want to make sure that I do everything right and don't do something stupid in the first practice. If I do make a mistake, I'd rather make one during practice than during qualifying or an actual race, that's for sure!

Like any athlete, for me practicing is about working out the kinks and sharpening my skill set to be the best I can be during the actual competition. Practices give me the chance to have space on the track. I am sometimes the only car out there, which is a totally different ex-perience from race day, when I am one of sometimes twenty or more cars on the track. My mind-set for practice runs is intense, but I know I am going out there to make one lap, test the track, talk to my team, pit, check the car, the engine, the tires, a leak check, whatever it takes to make sure the car is running supreme. I pit after one lap every time we make an engine change to make sure everything is running fine. Practice runs last about forty minutes. Sometimes there are one or two sessions on practice day, and I never miss them. No one does.

The goal is to go as fast as possible. Every lap is a push to go faster, faster, faster. If the car isn't turning correctly, I am trying to make it turn better. If the car is over-turning and the rear end wants to swing around, I am trying to settle it down. If the car isn't going through the corners with ease, I am making adjustments so it can go around a corner more freely. Any sign of a slide or slip, whether in the front or the end, needs to be handled by adjusting the car appropriately for the next lap.

When I'm out there, I'm just driving. I'm not consciously saying, "Okay, I've under-steered through this corner." There's very little self-talk going on while I'm on the track. Unless I'm crunched for time during a practice, I usually come into the pit and talk to my engineer and mechanic and tell them what I think the problem is. I must have excellent communication with Ray. I need to trust him and know that he can deliver a solution to any mechanical problem I might have. If he tells me he can't fix something, then I know it can't be done. I believe him. For the most part, there's always something that can be tweaked, tightened, and tuned to make the car drive better and go faster.

Ray is a literal engineering genius. There's a lot of trial and error, but Ray always has a positive outlook and is willing to try anything and everything to help me do better. If we make a change to the car and it performs worse, well, at least we know that during a crunch time, like in the middle of a race, not to do that again.

The only voices I hear when I'm driving are those of Ray and my spotter, Eric, whose voice I hear only during an actual race. He is perched above the track so he has a full view of the oval. His job is to watch the other cars on the track and report to me where everyone is. He literally acts as my eyes so I know when there's a car coming up on either side of me, or when there's a car right next to me. Some days are busier than others, but nothing was crazier than my 2005 Chicago race when he went through three batteries talking to me.

Danica Patrick

As I mentioned earlier, I have a very limited line of sight when I'm driving. I essentially can see from my hands, which are on the steering wheel, forward. I can't really see anything to the sides or behind me. When you hear the terms "driving blind" or "driving with blinders on," think of me in a racecar. My eyes are focused forward and can see only what is directly in front of me. I am trusting Eric with my life—literally. He is an amazing spotter.

When practice is over, I meet with Ray and the rest of my crew in the team truck for a formal debriefing. The truck is used to transport all of the cars and equipment needed for every race. Ray has taken a lot of notes on whatever I have communicated to him from the car; he has my individual lap times; he has meticulous notes on the various changes for each lap—what worked, what didn't; he'll talk about tire pressure, tire temperatures, engine stats, wing adjustments—all important information to use to help me go faster.

My 2005 season saw me setting the pace at a number of races. I often went into qualifying with the fastest lap time. As a rookie you feel more comfortable on the track when there are no other cars around. My lack of experience in my first IRL season was most evident during race conditions, with other cars around. I had to learn what to expect from my racecar, other drivers, and the constantly changing track and car conditions. Every time there is a full or empty fuel tank, new or old tires, and hot or cold temperatures, it affects the way the car handles on the track. I have a responsibility to my team and my sponsors to be ready to handle all of these changing elements, even as a rookie.

My sponsors are another important element behind the Rahal Letterman Racing team. In racing, sponsors are really business partners. They are using the sport as a means to improve their businesses. I have a responsibility to provide something of value to my sponsors. My performance is essential, but keeping them happy is the means to keeping their checkbook open so I can keep driving. Sponsors can spend several million dollars to sponsor a single car and a limited amount to sponsor an entire team, or they can spend as little as $100,000 for a small decal placed on my helmet or side pods. Without my sponsors, I'd be driving a cab—probably in New York City, where my aggressive driving skills would be best put to use. OK, seriously, my sponsors—including Argent Mortgage, my primary sponsor during my Toyota Atlantic program, who expanded its participation in motor sports by becoming a primary sponsor of our IRL team—are very important to my career.

Chapter FOUR

God Save the Queen

The conflict between the need to belong to a group and the need to be seen as unique and individual is the dominant struggle of adolescence.

—Jeanne and Don Elium

*I*t had been seven seasons since I raced my first kart. In 1997 my family and I went to the Indy 500 for the first time. I had participated in the Lyn St. James driver-development program and was really beginning to make a name for myself in racing. The program puts selected drivers through a barrage of tests designed to help young women drivers adapt and succeed in racing. It was at Lyn's suggestion that my family attended our first Indy 500. It was a good opportunity to meet potential sponsors and influential people as I prepared to make my jump from karts to Formula-style racing. Having been through the driver-development program with St. James, I gained a lot of experience and confidence in working with the media. I was preparing myself for what I could expect and how to get to the next level.

It was at the 1997 Indy 500 race that I first met John Mecom Jr., a Texas oil tycoon who fielded Graham Hill's Indy-winning car in 1966 and the one-time owner of the New Orleans Saints. We began talking about the racing culture in England. He explained to me that racing in England was difficult and challenging. It would be like going to drivers' boot camp, but it was an essential experience for any driver who wanted to turn professional. I was fourteen and too young to leave home. I didn't know the Mecoms would spend the next two years following my career.

Then, in 1999, I received a phone call from them asking my father and me to meet them in Indianapolis. This time we talked about me going to England to test a Formula Vauxhall car, an Indy-type car with a 150 hp engine that goes up to 150 mph. To make the trip to England, I enlisted the financial support of John Mecom III, the son of John Mecom Jr., who like his father also had a passion for racing. Not only did he partially pay for my ride in England, he became my manager. Ford Racing also took an interest in supporting my transition to racing Formula Fords.

By the time most of my friends were getting their driver's permits and driver's licenses, I had already been racing for six years. I knew that if I was going to fulfill my dream of becoming a professional racecar driver, my life would have to take a drastic turn. So while most kids my age were learning to navigate the highways and byways of life behind the wheel of their family car, at age sixteen I decided to quit high school, pack my bags, and move to England to pursue racing.

Thankfully, my parents understood that England offered better training and more opportunity for track time. Motor sports are more prestigious there than in the United States. Racers, especially young and less-experienced drivers who want to pursue open-wheel racing, hone their craft racing the European circuit. It's tougher and a lot more rigorous than the programs available in the United States. If I were truly pursuing my dream to someday win the Indy 500 or to race in Formula One, England was my fastest path to get there. So with my parents' permission and support, I was off to Milton Keynes, England, home to Jaguar Racing and the breeding ground of future motor sport champions.

I was living my dream.

> **The greatest gifts my parents gave to me . . . were their unconditional love and a set of values. Values that they lived and didn't just lecture about. Values that included an understanding of the simple difference between right and wrong, a belief in God, the importance of hard work and education, self-respect and a belief in America.**
>
> **—Colin Powell**

Danica Patrick

As I prepared to leave for England, my father sat me down and explained to me what I had to lose if I screwed up this opportunity. He was very strict when it came to making the right choices. He was aware that teenagers experiment with alcohol, and I was no exception. In all cases, there is simply no way for a person to drink and drive. But for me, not only would I lose my driver's license, I would lose my license to race and basically my future as a professional race-car driver. My father put the fear of God (worse, the fear of him!) in me by pointing out the cost of making a stupid decision to drink and drive or to even get into a car with someone who had been drinking. My dad conveyed a pretty simple concept: You drink, you drive, you crash, you break your neck, you ruin your career. I was sixteen years old. I had quit high school. I was leaving for Europe, and I thought I was old enough to make my own decisions. If I wanted to party, I would. Who would be there to check on me? I had to answer to myself, and, well, I was a teenager about to leave home for the first time. I guess we'd find out if my dad's advice was convincing enough.

By the time I left for England, I was well aware of the consequences of my actions if I made the wrong choices. There was a lot of peer pressure, which I never fell victim to. But for kids, there are always going to be temptations and choices to make. I had a bigger plan, a greater strength to just say "no." It was easy for me to tell my friends that I could randomly be subjected to drug tests by the racing league. If I tested positive, I'd be done—toast—finished—kaput. No drug was worth losing my ride. It became a game to dodge the people around me who were smoking pot and trying to get me high. I told them they could keep asking, but I would keep saying "no." I was never going to say "yes."

You don't have to be a racecar driver to understand that you always have something to lose if you get caught up in drugs or alcohol. Saying "no" is a test of your character and strength. Peer pressure and situations that tempt your good judgment are where the weak-minded get weeded (is that a bad pun to use here?) out from the strong. It's hard to grasp that when you are a teenager who still has a need for self-exploration and age-appropriate experimentation. But for me, it was an issue of discipline, which was an essential element in my success or failure as an athlete.

The only time I ever took a controlled substance was when I took Percocet for the pain I had after having my wisdom teeth pulled. I can admit that I liked it. I can see how someone might find taking a painkiller enjoyable. Enjoyable or not, I know not to abuse the drug. I have the discipline to take it only as prescribed because I know I have so much to lose if I were to abuse a prescriptive narcotic drug. I can be randomly drug-tested at any time. Racing is my drug of choice. There's no sense in risking everything I've worked so hard to achieve for a painkiller. There has always been a bigger picture to focus on than that momentary high, so it has always been easy for me to make the right choice. If you go against your conscience, you will always make the wrong choice. It's never right to get high. It's *never* right to drink and drive.

My parents did an excellent job at setting boundaries and guiding my sister and me in making the right choices, especially as teenagers. When you're young, you don't know any better, but your parents do. My parents had strict rules, but they had them for a reason.

I grew up in a home where pleasing my parents was just as important to me as winning races. They set high expectations for their children, and we were expected to live up to those standards. Even if we fell a little short, we were still doing pretty darn good. Those values they instilled showed me how I wanted to live my life. I didn't want to be a loser. Everything I was working toward was about winning. Losers make bad choices. Winners make the right choices. My parents brought me up with a one-track mind—to win.

I took my parents' wisdom to England with me. And I failed . . . miserably.

I got to England and realized there were no parents looking over my shoulder. I had free rein to do whatever I wanted with my time off the track. I began drinking on a more regular basis. European drivers had a totally different attitude than the one I grew up with when it came time to go to a pub. I was desperate to fit in with the guys, so I drank more than I did back home. I didn't party as much as some of the other drivers, but for me, who had successfully avoided the pitfalls of peer pressure before coming to England, my partying was damaging my chances of turning professional beyond any thought I could have had at the time.

All of the kids racing at Milton Keynes were living away from home, with no supervision, no real role models, and a lot of temptation. Alcohol in England was easily accessible. We all drank way more than we should have. Going to the pub after practice to have a few beers or cocktails was part of our English existence. It was as common as meeting someone for coffee at Starbucks which would have been a lot more age-appropriate back then as most of us were between sixteen and twenty years old. I can see that now, but in England I tried to just go with the flow to fit in and be accepted. I now know I had the option to not participate or make those choices, but at sixteen years old it was the only way I could feel that I belonged, It was a very fast life. I knew I had been making some lousy choices, but after a while I began to justify my behavior. It began to feel comfortable, even though instinctively I knew it was wrong.

A few months after I left home, my folks came to visit me in England. For the first time in my life, I couldn't wait for them to leave. I had parties to go to. I thought I was missing out on something if I missed a weekend with the gang. I learned very quickly that the party never changes. You don't miss anything new by missing a party. They're always the same. People drink, they dance, they get stupid, and then they puke or pass out.

My first year in England was a fast track to learning some of my greatest lessons in life. It definitely solidified my notion of right and wrong. Give someone, anyone, enough rope and he will hang himself. I was no exception. I am human and I was sixteen years old!

I left home and went to England to make the leap from racing go-karts to driving Formula-style cars in the Formula Vauxhall circuit. It wasn't an easy transition, especially when I became distracted. Bob Rahal refers to the Vauxhall and Formula Ford series as the "equivalent of automotive gang warfare." Racers go to England to be schooled in Formula racing. It's a ruthless prep league for drivers from all over the world who aspire to the Formula One racing circuit. Going to England and racing in these series was the best possible preparation for open-wheel racing. I had no idea what I was getting myself into, but I had to listen to my gut and just go for it.

England was tough on every level. The people I came into contact with were very old-fashioned in their thinking, especially in their sexist view of women and their role in society. A woman is supposed to cook, clean, and fetch a beer at her man's beck and call. This philosophy would be hard for me to swallow, especially when I discovered my host was the type of husband who ordered his wife around like she was a dog. I stared in disbelief every time I heard this man speak with such disrespect to his wife. I never heard my dad speak to my mother like that. This behavior was as foreign to me as being in a foreign country.

What had I gotten myself into? I thought he couldn't possibly be serious talking to her that way . . . but he was. He once made the grave mistake of asking me to "fetch" something for him. I responded, "Are your arms and legs broken? Go get it yourself!" I wasn't "fetching" anything for him—ever.

My first race in England was in the 1998 Winter Series. For some reason, the series was composed of only one race that year. Since this was my first race abroad, my sponsor and now manager, John Mecom III, attended this particular race. I was running eleventh out of fifteen cars racing during the practice runs. His advice to me was to go out there and push hard. They kept telling me that if I bent something, they could fix it. Go out there and try extra hard. So that's exactly what I did.

The track was damp from rain. If this particular track is wet, you have to lift the throttle in the back section of the track. If the track is dry, you're pretty much flat, which means the throttle is all the way down. Because of the conditions, I lifted a bit, but not enough, and slid right off the track, hitting a barrier and totaling the car! This was *not* the impression I had hoped to make on my bosses or the other racers that day.

I made the trip to England to race in the Winter Series, and it was over before I ever got into the race. I had tested my car for eight days—and before I had the chance to race my first race in England, I took myself out of the race.

When you race in England as a young person, there are no breaks given to wannabe drivers. It's a very hostile environment. The competition is fierce. What made it even more difficult for me was being a girl—the only girl. I knew I'd be dealing with the gender issue in England, but I had no concept of how extreme the bias and chauvinistic attitude would become nor the emotional impact it would have on me. It was slowly chipping away my self-esteem and building a wall around me that became almost impenetrable. I was turning inward and hiding my true self so I wouldn't have to face ridicule or rejection, despite performing at or above everyone else's level.

After one exceptionally good weekend of testing (I was a good 1.5 seconds faster than the next fastest driver), everyone was trying to figure out who was the fastest? My team owner responded by yelling loudly, in his cockney accent, "The frickin' girl's the fastest. Go out there and get your asses in gear. You're being beat by a girl!" I drove my ass off—and all I got was being referred to as the "frickin' girl?" His face was turning British flag red and spit flew from his chapped lips as he berated and browbeat the guys for being beaten by me. No wonder they hated me. If I were a guy out there, I'd be competition. As a girl, I was the reason they were being bitched at.

There's a different standard when you race Formula cars instead of karts. You're expected to be the best, not a weekend warrior. If this were the military, Milton Keynes, the city that was now our racing home, was West Point. It was a place that separated the men from the boys. Where did that leave me?

Yes, I was a young girl trying to fit in with all of the young boys, and we were aiming for a common goal. Being a girl described me, but it never defined me, at least not in my eyes. I wish I could say that was true in everyone else's eyes. The British engineers and mechanics turned a cold shoulder toward me, essentially allowing me to sink or swim on my own. I don't think my life was ever in danger, but my career rested in their hands. Worse yet, failing is one of my biggest fears; to me, it is like dying. Without the best equipment or the best team, I had no chance of competing on an equal level with the other drivers, who were given superior cars. Also, my ability to win a race was greatly impacted by a lack of support from the engineers and mechanics. They had little interest in seeing me break out as a driver. I would have been a "frickin' girl" taking the place of one of the boys, and as I've said, racing in England was definitely a good ol' boys club.

When you're a woman in a male-dominated world, there's always going to be apprehension and negativity from people. It's just the way it is, and as far as I can tell, it's not going to change any time soon. But it's OK, because through those experiences I became thick-skinned. Despite it all, I can now laugh off those idiotic comments—especially when I emerge victorious. Yes, success is the best revenge. Actions speak louder than words. There was nothing I could say that would prove my point better than going the fastest or winning races. In the end, the jerks who doubted me usually ended up just feeling stupid.

Word had gotten back to my managers that I was misbehaving.

They heard I was staying out too late and not taking care of my temple—I mean my body. Yes, excessive drinking does cause some weight gain. My managers were furious. They had a lot of money tied up in my racing, and they wanted to protect their investment as well as their good name. They were considering cutting me loose.

Although I had the financial backing of the Mecoms, I found myself with very little support or encouragement from them. The relationship was not what I would describe as warm and fuzzy. Their financial support certainly allowed me to be in England that first year, but the emotional toll of our relationship was brutal. I received no guidance and no support in getting my team's ass in gear. Without the proper equipment, I would continue to fail in my attempts to win races. I had the skill, the nerve, the desire, and the drive. I didn't have the car or a sponsor/manager who was willing to fight for me along the way. I was a ship with no ocean.

Perhaps I was young and naïve to believe that managers did more than offer financial support. I guess I expected more day-to-day support too. I was navigating this uncharted territory and was pretty much hanging out there all by myself. I asked for help. Every time I called John Mecom's office, I was assured they were doing all they could; they were seemingly always going into or just coming out of meetings about me. I would hang up the phone wondering if things would ever change. They never did.

I tried to make friends with the other drivers, but the truth is that they didn't want to be friends. We weren't in England to be buddies. We were there to become competitors. This wasn't summer camp; it was boot camp—serious boot camp, Navy SEAL style. This was no place for wimps, crybabies, or girly-girls (I borrowed that one from

Governor Arnold Schwarzenegger). I knew I didn't belong in the traditional sense, but I earned my place in England. I worked hard to get there.

That Which Does Not Kill You Makes You Stronger

Failure teaches success.

—Japanese saying

I vowed in England to never let my guard down in front of anyone. They would not break me; they would not make me cry. Three years of this type of thinking changed me. It hardened me. It made me stronger, but it also made me not like the person I was becoming. My overall experience during my three-year stay in England was lonely, depressing, and isolating, and yet it was a necessary period of time for teenage self-exploration and efforts toward finding, if not deepening, my inner strength. It was difficult for either of my parents to come to England and live with me because they were running the family business. Mom and Dad were both an integral part of the company, so neither could really afford to leave Illinois for an extended period of time without the business suffering, which would have impacted my racing because they were still financially supporting me and paying a good portion of my expenses when I was living abroad. It wasn't uncommon for kids my age who went to England to race to be on their own. The team watched over us to some degree, though they were hardly parental figures. At sixteen or seventeen years old, we were pretty self-sufficient. I could certainly take care of myself, even if I didn't always make the best choices along the way.

Whenever I came home for a visit, my parents commented on how different I was. My mom kept telling me I was tougher, harder— that I had grown colder. She didn't mean any of this in a good way. They were worried. How would this impact my future and my ability to connect on an interpersonal level?

I am what I am now because of that time in my life. I've never been a pushover, but those years in England definitely contributed to my need to prove that I am a worthy competitor. Looking back, I guess I should be grateful, but on so many levels I resent those years for the pain and the angst of being far away from home, separated from my family and friends. I was very much alive on the outside, but on the inside I felt like I was dying a slow, painful, lonely death.

Adversity reveals and shapes character. It weakens the weak and strengthens the strong

—Anonymous

Despite the difficulty of living so far away from my family and friends, and because of all that I learned during those dark years, England is a time in my life that I am also grateful for because I truly believe that I would not be where I am today had I not lived through those years. Looking back on it now, I realize that those were the years in my life when I learned the most about myself. I grew and experienced so many transitional moments—not just as a racer, but as a young girl making my inevitable transformation into womanhood. Even though I was alone most of the time, I am a stronger person today because I learned to be independent, learned to entertain myself, and learned to appreciate and then strengthen the trust and bond between myself and the people who are closest to me.

> **I'm starting to wonder what my parents were up to at my age that makes them so doggoned suspicious of me all the time!**
>
> **—Margaret Blair**

I came home after my first year in England, and I was different. I'd been on my own, living abroad, and had forgotten that my parents had rules I was expected to abide by. I was seventeen years old and thought I was immune to their restrictions. I was not. One thing my parents strongly encouraged me to do after my first year in England was to get my GED. I called it my "Good Enough Diploma," but it really meant completing my high school education. Even though I was sure that I would become a racecar driver, how could I really be certain? It was a good idea to finish high school, because what if I didn't succeed? What would my plan be then? No one was going to hire a washed-up racecar driver with no diploma.

If I needed any proof of that, when I got home after being in England my first season my parents made me apply for several jobs to earn some extra money for the upcoming holidays. I got a part-time job at the Limited Too. The Christmas music at the mall starts playing moments after you've finished your last bite of Thanksgiving turkey. It drove me nuts. Despite the hectic holiday rush, it was good to spend some time at home with my friends and family before I had to leave for my second season in January. For a moment, I was a regular teenager. My life consisted of working, studying, and hanging out with my friends. It was fun for a while, but a vast change from life in the fast lane.

On my parents' wedding anniversary, as they planned an evening out, I decided I would meet up with some friends at a party later that same night. My parents were always very aware of where I was going and who I would be with when I went out with friends. Somewhere around four o'clock in the morning, I decided to drive home with a bunch of my girlfriends. My house was less than two miles from the party. It was two stop signs and one left turn away. I opened the garage door, and my mother's car was parked in my spot. My friends freaked out, scared my parents would bust us for being out so late. My attitude was, "Who cares?" I thought living abroad meant I could do whatever I wanted and that I was above their wrath. That was clearly not the case.

My parents had called home several times during the evening to check on my sister and to see if I was home yet. Brooke, who was now fifteen, tried to cover for me, saying I was in bed sleeping, which was not true. My parents weren't buying her story. Their anger turned to worry when I still hadn't come home by the time they walked through the door after midnight. My father immediately asked my friends to leave, but not before confronting us on whether we'd been drinking. We denied it, but the truth is, we had been drinking. I was in trouble—big trouble.

I was grounded for a month. Since my parents had made me get a job, my life pretty much consisted of going to work and coming right home. I knew it was going to be a long, long, winter.

It had been almost a month since I was grounded. I was days away from being in the clear to go out again when I received an unexpected phone call on my cell. I was about to leave work when my parents called and told me to come right home instead of going to Brooke's soccer game, as planned.

"We need to talk to you."

Those are six dreaded words for any teenager to hear—but when it came to my parents, it *never* meant anything good.

What could they know? I was terribly nervous. Something really bad was about to happen. I had no idea what was coming, but I knew I was screwed.

I drove home, my mind running wild. What did I do? And how did they find out?

They dropped their news like a Scud missile. Kaboom! My world was about to implode.

"The Mecoms called. They want nothing to do with you anymore. They heard you've been going out too much and not focusing on your racing. They want no part of that lifestyle for one of their drivers."

Gulp.

And then the tears started. I began to cry so hard I couldn't catch my breath.

"I'll do anything to fix this. Anything!" I hysterically screamed through my desperate gasps for air.

"Have you been doing things you shouldn't have?"

"No."

"Don't lie to us, Danica. We'll make a couple of phone calls and find out the truth anyway."

"OK. Yes."

My parents were beside themselves. What had happened to me in England? Who did I think I was, living my life this way? I was lying, drinking, and irresponsible. This is not how they had raised me. I was humiliated, embarrassed, and so sad that I had let them down. Worse than that, I had let myself down. All of my hard work, and I may never race again? The very thought was excruciating.

Still crying, I pleaded for their forgiveness. "I am so sorry. What can I do to fix this? Tell me! I'll do whatever it takes."

I begged my parents not to abandon me on this. My father's way of teaching me a lesson was to let me figure out how to get myself out of situations I created. It was tough love, but effective love. I didn't understand that as well back then as I do today.

I wasn't perfect. I was certainly no angel, but the people I was hanging around with in England were doing a lot worse than I was, so I never saw my behavior as being "bad" or "unacceptable," at least not in the moment. If you judge yourself in terms of the worst, you base yourself on the worst. Judge yourself in terms of the best, and you will rise to the level of being the best. Looking back on it today, I realize I was way out of line. I was a child living in an adult world. I wasn't ready for a lot of the temptations that were placed in front of me. But through those experiences, I learned to be stronger and wiser in my decisions in the future.

My first task at hand was convincing the Mecoms not to let me go. I made the hardest phone call of my life. I told them I would change.

Danica Patrick

I wanted to get my life back on track and was willing to do whatever they wanted to not lose my ride. They said they'd have to think about it. I promised I'd change. I told them I would do anything to go back to England. Despite the emotional misery, I knew that racing there was a vital and important experience for my future. I had totally messed things up. I made promises to them in that phone call, and I intended to keep them. I needed an attitude adjustment—and fast. My parents were hard on me. My dad was disappointed that I had gained weight, which was a direct result of drinking. I quit—and began working out. My mother and I got up at five o'clock in the morning and drove thirty minutes to a gym in Rockford to take an aerobics class. Until I started exercising with my mom, I had lied all the time about the frequency of my workouts. (The funny thing is, these days I'm more inclined to deny how much I really do work out!)

My motivation was to show my parents and managers that I was serious about redirecting my life. I wanted—no, needed—to prove to them that I was in racing for the right reasons. I was committed and would do whatever it took to make sure they all knew it.

Chapter FIVE

My Big Fat European Victory

There is always room at the top.

—Daniel Webster

The Mecoms finally agreed to let me do a second season in England, but with the condition that I live with a family there in virtual lockdown. I had no privileges. I wasn't allowed to stay the night anywhere. It was mandatory to be home for dinner every night. In addition to the limited financial support the Mecoms were still giving me, I also garnered the financial support of the Ford Motor Company, which offset a good deal of my expenses of living and racing in Europe. To get the Mecoms to take me back, I had to get serious about my racing, and that's just what I did. I spent the season working hard and sharpening my skills, and despite all of the challenges of driving with less-than-perfect equipment, I finally showed everyone who doubted me that I was worthy.

Well done is better than well said.
—Benjamin Franklin

I know that England is a gray, gloomy, usually dark and rainy place. But all of my days there weren't so bad. Toward the tail end of my second full season in England, the sun finally metaphorically came out on one particularly memorable race weekend. Even though it had rained the whole weekend, my heart, if only for a moment, was filled with sunshine.

The Formula Ford Festival is a main event for the Formula Ford Series; more than 100 cars enter for this particular race. Prior to the race I had been driving secondary for the Haywood Racing Team. I was supposed to be getting a lot of help from them setting up my car. They selected what shocks I should run, the sway bars, tire pressures, and such. My second season hadn't gone that well, but at the end of the year I was, as promised, promoted to the primary Haywood team. My "gift" for being bumped up to the team before racing in the Formula Ford Festival was Anthony Davidson's old chassis from his past season, which is a lot like using someone's old baseball glove—it might feel broken in, but it isn't going to fit your hand like it does the rightful owner's. Anthony Davidson also raced for Haywood Racing and was the 1999 and 2000 Winter Series Champion.

I decided to take that old car, go out there, and do the best I could. I raced hard and fast all day. I finished nothing short of fifth all weekend long out of two qualifying runs and four races. All of my other teammates had their own cars, and I was given someone's hand-me-down. On race day, I started ninth overall. I raced fast that day. I had worked my way up to sixth place when a red flag came out. The race stopped, but when we started again I began to think I was doing OK for starting ninth out of more than 100 cars! I was racing in sixth place. That was pretty good—far better than I had raced all season.

As I sat on the starting grid, strapped into my car waiting for the race to restart, something in my memory said, "Wait a minute!" Just then, I remembered a dream I had in which I was in the same situation, but that dream hadn't ended well, so I decided to channel all of my energy into a positive direction. I always believed that dreams predict future events. The dreams we remember can help us navigate through tight situations, but it's the dreams we cannot recall that really unveil our destiny.

This wasn't the end—I could do better. I knew I could. Since when was I ever satisfied with sixth place?

"*This* is your opportunity to do better. Go for it!"

As the race started again, all of the drivers were bunched up, I told myself to *not* look back. As the green flag dropped, I never looked in my rearview mirror again. I looked forward, passing car after car after car until I found myself racing in third position.

There were two laps to go.

The two leaders came together at the first corner. One spun in the dirt and went off the track. I'm in second! As we made our last lap that day, I finished in second place at the Formula Ford Festival in England—the highest-ever finish for an American in the event. The last racer to do almost as well was Danny Sullivan in 1974, and he finished fourth! Maybe there's something to be said for an old, worn-in baseball glove, after all!

Formula Ford

Established in England in 1967, Formula Ford has been an international entry-level racing series and often a developmental stepping-stone for young drivers on the road to Formula One racing. Its original aim was to create a low-cost entry for drivers into motor sports and initially it was established that the total cost of the Formula Ford cars were not to exceed £1,000 (approx. $1,800). However, over time the rule has been done away with. The relative light weight of the single-seater class cars allows their Ford 1600 cc "Kent" engines to push them to top speeds of approximately 140 mph. For maximum traction during various weather conditions, the Formula Ford cars use grooved racing tires and are equipped with complete racing-car suspension designs. Aerodynamic devices such as "wings" are not allowed, which cuts down on down-force and also provides the cars with a unique appearance. Formula Ford is widely considered to be one of the most important formulas outside Formula One. Other similar formulas include Formula BMW and Formula Renault.

> I like things to happen; and if they don't
> happen, I like to make them happen.
> —*Winston Churchill*

What I discovered after that race was that up to this point, I hadn't been given the opportunity to drive the right cars. Despite the second-hand vehicle, it was better than any car I had driven during my first couple of years abroad. Given the right vehicle, I was able to perform at a higher level. This wasn't a one-race fluke. I had performed well all weekend, and it was in great part due to the quality of the car I was driving. Why didn't anyone see this before that weekend? Even though I did really well that day, still no one gave me the credit due. This realization left me frustrated and confused.

I was angry that it took two years for someone to provide me with competitive equipment. It was such a waste of time and confidence, not to mention the sadness I carried with me during those years: all of my second-guessing myself, and the perception of others that my lack of performance was because of a lack of skill rather than a lack of equipment. This took away important years that could have built me up, made me a better racer, and given me even more opportunities to grow as a driver. And yet, despite all of the angst and disappointment, I remain grateful for those experiences because they taught me to survive and even thrive in whatever car I was given, which made me a better driver.

My experiences in England taught me how to deal with difficult people, characteristics, and circumstances. I learned whom I could trust and whom not to trust, and in the end one of my greatest lessons was learning you need to clear the path you walk on for yourself because no one else is really interested in clearing it for you. They have their own paths. Professionally, there was no one there to handle the challenges that arose or the constant struggle of trying to get behind the wheel of the right car, the one that would allow me to break out as a racer. There was no one watching the mechanics working on my car, no one directing them to make the car better or faster. I've never been a mechanic. I don't know what they are supposed to be doing.

You have to be able to trust your team. If your team doesn't back you, support you, and stand behind you in every way, you will fail. I spent years in go-karting, where people were honest, changes were made, and a genuine team effort was put forth by everyone connected to my career. It was all about my support team. My father was my mechanic, my engineer, my coach, and my manager. He would never leave me out there on a limb to fend for myself. He stopped at nothing to see to it that I had the tools to race the fastest in each and every race. That simply wasn't the case when I went to England.

Chapter SIX

What's a Girl to Do?

Everyone has talent. What is rare is the
courage to follow the talent to the dark place
where it leads.

—Erica Jong

Aside from racing, my second season in England was mostly
spent alone, watching movies in my room. All of that isolation
added to my loneliness and depression, which had all but immediately set in again after I returned from the States. I started the season
watching Adam Sandler comedies, but as the season progressed, I
found myself being drawn to darker films, such as *Cruel Intentions*.

Danica Patrick

My family came to visit me a couple of times during the year; unlike in my first year, when I couldn't wait to see them go, this year it grew harder each time they left.

The only social interaction I had was with the boys I raced against. I only had one girlfriend in England, but she lived two hours away and worked, so seeing her was difficult. Girls need their girls. That's why I especially cherished the trips my sister, Brooke, made to visit because she was easy to be with and I could let my guard down a bit when she was around and just be one of the girls. For some reason I just didn't click with the girls I met in England.

Alienation is a form of living death.
—Martin Luther King Jr.

To be completely honest, I've never really been a girl's girl. I've spent my entire life as one of girls who is one of the boys. I'd been slapped in the face so many times by the reality of living like one of the guys that I think I lost perspective on connecting with women. I wasn't a boy. I am a girl. Living like one of the guys was a method of survival in England. I hid my girly-girl side in order to fit in, and for the first time in my life I was avoiding standing out in the crowd. I missed out on so much by suppressing who I really was. I avoided wearing pink and purple or anything too frilly, just to ensure I wouldn't be judged as being too feminine.

I never wanted to be a "face first" girl, lest anyone get the wrong impression of me because I had manicured nails or wore pretty dresses. I was ridiculously protective of my femininity. I didn't want the guys to think we had nothing in common to talk about. Racing was our bond, and it was the sole connection to getting along, at least for me. The fact that I was a girl and they were boys was moot. I wanted to be a guy's girl. I wanted friends. I needed their approval. I was insecure and very afraid of being rejected. I'd do whatever it took to fit in, even if it meant hiding my true self. What a mistake.

I like to think of anything stupid I've done as a learning experience. It makes me feel less stupid.

—P. J. O'Rourke

Teenage boys can be pretty mean to a girl who is messing around in "their" sport. But they are just boys being boys. I began to date, which didn't help matters much. I met my first boyfriend in England during the Winter Series. It was a short-lived romance once I met one of his closest friends, who caught my eye.

Rule to remember: Never date your boyfriend's best friend or roommate.

The new boy stole my heart. He was an excellent racer—funny, nice, and very handsome. Before I moved to England, I had a tendency to wear my heart on my sleeve. I was very open with my emotions and communicated very well, especially when it came to my personal feelings for someone. I'd sit for hours at a time and pour my heart out to a boy I liked. I was way too open, a lesson that later would bite me in the butt.

I was having fun with my new boyfriend. I told my soon-to-be ex that I needed to focus on my racing, that our relationship was interfering with my focus. I was sixteen years old. I had no idea how to break up with someone. It was probably a bad move! Honesty really is the best policy.

Later that season, the two guys returned to England and became roommates. After avoiding going to their house for as long as I could, I eventually had to tip my hand that I knew both because I wanted to spend time with my new boyfriend. So much for the story that I needed to focus on my racing. Knowing what I know now, I would have made different decisions on how to handle things, but I was sixteen years old and had very little experience with relationships.

I learned about heartbreak in the relationship I was choosing to pursue. In the beginning I had no idea he had another girlfriend. I began to figure it out after he made several weekend trips to his hometown without me. After six months of his weekends away, I figured out that there was, in fact, someone else. I was hurt and sad and extremely disappointed. I realized he was never going to break up with her, though he told me he would over and over. There was no choice anymore. Our relationship had to end.

Just what I needed! In addition to all of the angst I was already feeling from being away from home, and being away from my friends and family again, I was now facing my first real breakup. Here I was, this strong, unflappable young woman, and it felt as though my world was falling apart . . . over a guy! I was almost eighteen, but I still felt like a wounded little girl.

After we broke up, I was incredibly lonely. I was struggling with my racing and living in what I perceived to be a maximum-security prison for teenagers. Ugh! I didn't think life could be any worse.

I allowed myself to be treated like crap by this guy. I took it. I accepted it.

What part of my so-called "high self-esteem" had this little fracture in it that made me think this was OK?

Was I so desperate for acceptance in England that I took it any way it came, even at my own expense?

Did I think it was OK to be with someone while he had another girlfriend?

Hey, great idea. Not! If I wanted to set myself up for hurt and disappointment, then I ought to go right ahead and keep seeing boys with girlfriends. But that isn't what I wanted. It was a living hell. Really, what else could I expect in that situation? It's really easy now for me to see how foolish I was being, but back then I actually thought I was making the right choice to be with someone who was dating another girl. It should have been a sign that I was miserable, confused, and feeling pretty bad for myself. I should have been able to recognize that my choices were not helping my self-esteem—they were destroying it. Easy to say now, impossible to understand at seventeen.

Here's the deal. If your boyfriend (or girlfriend) has another girlfriend (or boyfriend,) you are not his girlfriend (or boyfriend!). It's pretty simple. That doesn't change as you get older either. It's a steadfast rule. You can't be someone's girlfriend if he already has another girlfriend.

If a man isn't making you his one and only, leave him. Break up. Dump his sorry ass. It's so easy for me to say now, but I couldn't see my way clear to feel that way at sixteen. When you're young, you'll find any excuse to be optimistic. I wish the book *He's Just Not That Into You* had been available back then. It ought to be mandatory reading for every young girl who is starting to date.

I wanted a boyfriend so badly I was willing to wait for him. I made excuses in my own mind why I ought to wait. I acted like it didn't bother me, but in reality I spent many nights crying myself to sleep to sad songs on the radio. You can't *make* someone be your boyfriend. God knows I tried.

It wasn't long after we broke up that I decided I wanted to find a nice guy or none at all. I didn't date much after that. I wouldn't put up with being treated with disrespect. I didn't want to make poor choices that would impact my self-esteem. Relationships that chip away at your self-image impact your whole life. You lose perspective—especially at sixteen or seventeen years old.

Let's face it. Most of us won't marry our high school sweethearts. I put way too much emphasis on the relationships I was having at that age instead of thinking, "I'm too young to settle down. Move on and have fun!"

After my previous boyfriend, I made the decision to avoid, at all cost, the bad boys, the guys who could hurt me.

Except for this one . . .

In 1995, while at a go-kart race with Lyn St. James in North Carolina, I met a nice, shy guy. My father actually got along with him, which was a miracle. They had an instant bond. Usually guys were intimidated by my dad. Not this one. He had spunk and was very funny, which drew all of us to him. Prior to leaving for England, much to my surprise and delight I discovered he would also be there racing Formula Ford. This would turn out to be a stroke of dating misfortune for me.

Rule to remember: Stop dating racecar drivers.

We started hanging out. We spent lots of time together going to movies, having dinners, and watching television at his flat in London. I began to feel comfortable with our relationship, so much so that I started to think of him as my boyfriend.

It had been months. We had sort of been seeing each other, but we never officially called each other "boyfriend" and "girlfriend." I made my own assumption, but I was wrong. That was the hardest part. I never knew where I stood. I thought I felt safe and secure that this boy wouldn't hurt me. But it turned out that he could and he did. We decided to go away to our home countries for Christmas and not start dating until we came back in January for the new season. I was sure I could trust him. I was wrong.

And then it was January, the beginning of my third year in England, but it would be the same old story as my first two years, at least as far as the boys in my life were concerned.

The boy I was "certain wouldn't hurt me" came back to England with his girlfriend, yet another woman I never knew existed.

Once more, I was emotionally crushed. This was the second guy to do this to me in two years.

That relationship was the final straw. The worst part for me was that some of the guys were friends, and boys stick together, which meant I was left sitting alone on my couch watching more episodes of *Sabrina the Teenage Witch* than I would like to admit. I learned that I do not want to be in an uncertain relationship. I absolutely didn't want to be in a relationship with false hope or expectations. I definitely didn't want to be someplace I wasn't wanted. But again, I was so lonely I was willing to put myself in a situation where I could be hurt rather than sitting alone in my bedroom.

Worse yet, I began to wonder what was wrong with me?

Why didn't these guys want me to be their "girlfriend"?

I became so self-conscious.

Wasn't I pretty enough?

Was I too fat?

Was it my body?

I knew I was a good person. I was fun to be around.

What was I lacking that the guys I dated in my teens wanted?

The whole experience changed the way I thought about guys and their motivations. I was much more careful with my heart. I would not give it to someone who wasn't going to take care of my heart as if it were his own. I just wanted someone to love me as much as I loved him. That's all! It doesn't seem like it should be that hard to find, but it was. This ripping and tearing of the heart left me single and wounded for five years. I know . . . it's a long time. I found that being alone ended up being a lot easier than trying to sew my heart, emotions, and confidence back together.

I never had a real boyfriend before I met my husband. I had a lot of disappointing relationships. I was the girl boys liked to hang out with—their buddy, their pal, their chum—but mostly I was a pretty desperate girl looking for love. It was pitiful.

Looking back, I was just young and wrapped up in the moment, but that was part of being a teenager. Everything, especially relationships and my raging emotions, seemed bigger than Mount Everest. I couldn't understand what was wrong with me. I began a downward spiral that would take me three years to come out of. I turned inward. I became unapproachable, cold, thick-skinned. My parents tell me I've never been the same since England.

Chapter *SEVEN*

What About Bob?

Success isn't permanent, and failure isn't fatal.

—Mike Ditka

My 2000 and 2001 seasons were spent racing in England for the Team Haywood satellite team Andy Welch Racing. The year 2001 was my third year abroad and the one that taught me the most. My results weren't there, but coming so close in the 2000 Formula Ford Festival more than made up for all of my pain and suffering so far. I had made a lot of progress in my driving, and it was beginning to show. My presence was undeniable. People were taking notice.

Testing at the beginning of the season went well. Despite the lackluster equipment, I felt I had done everything I could to prepare myself for the upcoming 2001 season. I like to call 2001 "the season that never was." My frustration with Haywood Racing had become unbearable for everyone. No one could convince them to step up, not even after the Formula Ford Festival. It made no sense. I was bitter and confused. Though my father did everything he could from a distance, being cautious not to be too overbearing, he too understood that I wasn't being treated fairly. His frustration only continued to exacerbate and fuel my own.

The Mecoms tried to help me, but it was too difficult to fight on my behalf when they were not in England. So I was hanging out there without decent equipment or substantive support in confronting the team that wasn't using me to the best of my abilities. They finally suggested I come home and wait for a better situation if I was that dissatisfied with the team. What were they talking about? Me? Throw in the towel? Call it a race? It was uncharacteristic and unimaginable, especially with a race the next day.

I couldn't believe the Mecoms were telling me not to show for a race! This was just unthinkable. I had never missed a race. It was unprofessional. It was immature. It was against every ounce of how I live, think, eat, and breathe. The mere suggestion, let alone the reality of it, was one of the most disheartening moments of my career. My integrity was being called out, as were my beliefs and my reputation. All I had worked for—was I willing to throw all of that away? If I left England, if I didn't show up for this race, if I let down my team—in my mind, it equaled career suicide. But my managers felt this was the best solution to solve my disenchantment with the team. The order came down at midnight the night before—*Do not go to the race tomorrow.* Nothing like waiting until the last minute, and that's coming from me, the queen of procrastinators! The responsibility of calling the owner of Team Haywood and telling him I wasn't coming to the race fell on my shoulders. This was not a phone call I wanted to make, nor was it a phone call I should have made. At the very least, my managers could have taken that burden off me. They did not. Fingers trembling, I dialed the phone. I could barely squeak the words from my mouth.

I had never felt as empty or disappointed as I did that next morning. It was a strange feeling, knowing there was a race I had prepared for but was not driving in by choice. It felt wrong. I felt lost, sad, hurt, worried, and scared. I was supposed to be doing something and I wasn't doing it. There was someplace I was supposed to be and I was sitting at home. Thank God, my sister was with me. She made those uncertain days fun and tolerable. She helped me pack my bags, and we flew home. At least I was home. That was the silver lining to my otherwise stormy existence living abroad.

So I came back to the States in 2001 after racing only five Formula Ford races. I went several months without driving, something I hadn't done since I was ten years old and something I didn't expect. My first glimmer of hope was discovering that my manager had started Heritage Motor Sports, an Indy racecar team, with Jim Rathman Jr. I thought they set the team up to offer me a ride, to give me the chance to make my transition to IndyCar racing. I thought wrong.

My unexpected break in training gave me a lot of time to think about my time abroad, the people I was dealing with, whom I could trust, and how to clear the path for my future. I was certain that from that point forward I would work only in a situation where I was teamed up with the best people in the business. I never again wanted to find myself in a situation where my performance was impacted by people who didn't believe in me, my talent, my skill, and my ability to deliver.

Racing in England was a low point in my career. I knew things had to start changing—meaning they had to get better. How long could the negative cycle last? I felt things would turn around. I had to believe they would.

Although we still had a contract, I never drove for John Mecom again. He was a very honorable and fair man. I clearly needed to move on if I had any hope of breaking into the American racing scene and John let me do that. I was hanging by a thread. No sponsor. No ride. No direction.

I did a little bit of testing for Ford as a way to try to enlist their support stateside since they had helped sponsor my last two years in England. I tested a U.S. Auto Club midget car prepared by chassis guru Bob East. Testing that car was my first real oval-track experience since I had quit racing karts. My racing in England was completely done on road courses. Beyond that test, my father and I spent as much time as we could at tracks, looking for a ride. We laced up our sneakers and began walking the track paddocks at various venues, going to as many races as we could and talking to anyone who would listen. We were looking for a Formula Atlantic ride, which seemed like the obvious progression for me professionally. I shook a lot of hands and asked a lot of people if I could test-drive for them. Dad and I almost became annoying in our effort to get a test, let alone secure a ride. We spent so much time at tracks with nothing to do, no one to talk to, and nowhere to go . . . except the bathroom, which became an instant ten-minute time filler. It became like a joke between us. We'd look at each other and ask, "Hey, you gotta go?" Even if the answer was really no, I always answered, "Sure, this will take up some time." And you never know who you might meet in the bathroom.

On one very memorable trip to the loo, I ran into a woman who owned a Formula Atlantic team. Oddly, she had a video camera and asked everyone in the ladies' room if she could tape them getting slapped on the butt. I'm not generally a desperate woman, but that day I took one for the team! And believe it or not, I still didn't get a ride!

Testing a racecar is expensive. After ten years of racing and three years of racecar boot camp in England, my parents had all but tapped out their personal resources. Everything in England cost nearly double what it cost in the States, and I had developed power-shopping skills by then too. Though sponsors pay for about half of the expenses, car owners were commanding as much as $1 million from prospective drivers. There was simply no way my family could afford that kind of money. In a tightened economy and a post-9/11 environment, corporate money wasn't flowing as freely as it had been a year or two earlier. My only option was to find someone who had the resources, the clout, and the ability to put me behind the wheel.

Bob Rahal was the guy—he just needed me to prove to him I was worthy of his time and effort. I had met him a couple of times over the years. He's a behind-the-scenes looker. He's subtle when he's scouting a driver. He set up a test with a BMW team called PTG. Tom Milner owns and runs PTG. He's known for being pretty tough on his drivers, but I never saw that side. He was always extremely nice to me. He was so impressed with my performance that he gave me a ride on his team. For the next year I was *finally* a paid professional driver. It would be an ironic false start. The BMW cars I was hired to drive were never allowed to race because of unexpected new Series rules, which made Milner's particular cars ineligible to race in the American Le Mans Series. I was a paid driver with no car, no races, and all the time in the world to continue looking for an open-wheel ride.

And then in 2002, Bob gave me a shot driving in the Toyota Pro/Celebrity Race in Long Beach, California. That was the race that finally turned the U.S. racing tide for me professionally. It wasn't the Indy 500, but I was in a situation where I had to perform, and if I wanted to make a name for myself in America, I knew this race would be the perfect opportunity to go out there and get noticed.

Pressure?

What pressure?

There were 100,000 pairs of eyes staring down at me from the stands, but the only person I wanted to impress that day was Mr. Rahal. I felt good about the race—so good, in fact, that I made a small wager with Tommy Kendall, a former Trans Am champion and winner of the Pro/Celebrity race. During the drivers' meeting prior to the race, Tommy suggested to me that we "raise the stakes a little. Whoever wins the race gets to lead the other down pit lane by a leash and collar." Tommy should have known better. I knew that the best way to quiet my critics was by beating them. Was Tommy trying to intimidate me with that bet or trying to be funny? In the end, it backfired on him.

I went on to lead the field, which included Tommy Kendall and Sarah Fisher, from flag to flag, and become the first professional female to win the event. That was awesome—but not as awesome as leading Tommy, who stands around 6'4", around pit lane on the end of my leash!

Toyota Atlantic Championship

Sponsored by Toyota since 1988, the Toyota Atlantic Championship is a top developmental single-seat open-wheel racing series that competes all across the United States, Canada, and Mexico. The cars are manufactured by Swift Engineering and possess Toyota 4A-GE 1.6-liter, four-cylinder engines that produce speeds in excess of 165 mph. Since its first event in 1974, the series has raced on street courses, permanent road circuits, and short ovals ranging from 60 to 100 miles in length. The minimum cost for a team racing the entire twelve-race season is over $650,000. After competing in the Toyota Atlantic Championship Series, drivers often then move up to the Indy Racing League. Unfortunately, in 2006 Toyota did not return as a title sponsor and the new owner, Champs Car World Series, LLC changed the name to the Champ Car Atlantic Championship.

After Long Beach, I tested in an Indy Lights car, and again I did really well. I also tested a Toyota Atlantic car. Most of my high-profile and important tests were being produced by Bob Rahal, so he was able to track my progress and my results. I was slowly showing him I could do it. A lot of "lookie loos" hang around a race track. You never know who is real and who is not. People make all sorts of promises they can't keep, just to get close to drivers, especially up-and-coming drivers. A guy named Troy was one of those guys I saw from time to time around the track. He too was taking notice of my progress and potential. One day, to my surprise, I received a call from him saying he had a sponsor who would pay my budget for the upcoming Toyota Atlantic Championship Series if I could get a letter of intent that I had a ride with Team Rahal Racing (it wasn't yet Rahal Letterman Racing).

Up to this point, I had tested several times for Bob, but he hadn't indicated one way or the other whether he was truly interested in me as a driver for his team. I thought about the situation and decided I had absolutely nothing to lose by asking. I hoped and prayed Troy wasn't yanking my chain with his "sponsor." But I thought, "Hey, let's see if Bob is serious about me." I couldn't be afraid to ask the question or hear his answer, regardless of the outcome.

After so many race weekends spent walking around, virtually begging for a chance, my stamina and faith were being tested. On this particular weekend, the race at the Milwaukee Mile was only a forty-five-minute drive from our house. I told my dad I didn't want to go. I was sick of being disappointed, shot down, and rejected. I was actually beginning to think nobody was ever going to give me the chance I needed. The one I had earned and deserved. But in the end, my conscience got the best of me, as it usually does. Understanding my frustration, my dad suggested we make the drive but promised we'd stay for only an hour. So we saddled up and drove to Milwaukee. My only mission was to ask Bob Rahal what his intentions were for my future—and if he really believed I could do it. With the potential of a full sponsor, I knew I'd, at the very least, be able to get his attention. I was a little worried he was going to turn me down cold. No one had really given me any indication

Bob was quite *that* interested. We got to the track, and within forty-five minutes I spotted Bob. I swallowed hard, looked him right in the eyes, and said, "So, I've been told that we apparently have a full sponsor for the car if I can get a letter of intent from you to run Atlantic next year."

"Yeah. All right. OK." That was his response.

Whoa. My jaw was open and I was in a slight state of shock. Why hadn't I asked him this sooner? Two weeks later I was in Laguna Seca, at a press conference arranged by Team Rahal, announcing my new relationship with the team. I was officially racing in the Toyota Atlantic Series.

I stopped calling John Mecom after that. I figured if he wanted to talk, he would call me. The Mecoms were reasonable, honorable men. They helped me get started and I am grateful for that support, but I never heard from them again.

I know Bob Rahal was taking a chance in offering me a ride. He didn't have to take me on. He's in this relationship for all of the right reasons. I believe he really wants what's best for me. I had never experienced that kind of support from a team owner until I raced for Bob. I think he gave me my ride because he was given the same opportunity by Jim Trueman when he was a young driver starting out. Mr. Trueman made Bob work hard for his ride. He had him move to Columbus, Ohio, where he lived, to work more closely with the team. This was the way Bob did it, and therefore it would be the way that I would do it too.

I know his intention with me was to give something back to the sport. He wanted to give someone the same opportunity he had been

given. It was his way of passing the torch, and I was the very lucky recipient of his goodwill.

Bob knew he'd have to defend me, my skill, my ability, my gender. And for the first time since I was driving go-karts, I had someone in my corner, someone other than my mom and dad, who believed in me as much as I believed in myself. I now work for a team and have bosses I *want* to please. I have a mentor—someone who wants to teach me everything he knows so I can be the best driver I can be. When he says something, I listen.

It's taken me a while to recognize that I don't know everything! I guess that comes with age and experience.

I have matured and am smart enough to know that someone like Bob isn't going to waste his breath or his time feeding me nonsense or misinformation. He's a man of few words, and he talks when it is important. He's a wonderful mentor and role model.

Early in our relationship Bob took me aside and offered me the following advice. He told me that I have to drive every race like I've got something to prove. He explained that's when true racers drive their best and that it makes them try their hardest. He explained to me that people will always come along with one goal: *to beat me.* "As long as you keep that fire in your belly, and race like you have something to prove every time, things will go well for you. Just keep making me look good, D (that's what he calls me). Keep making me look like I'm the smartest man in racing!"

Lyn St. James once referred to my "fire in the belly" during an interview when I was fourteen years old. She recognized I had that spark—that enthusiasm and burning desire that eats away inside you for a cause, a job, a sport, or whatever it is you're passionate about.

Fire in the belly is what drives me to be successful. Anyone who has that sensation inside them knows what I am talking about. It's an indescribable feeling that drives us to do better and be better at anything we do or love. It's the reason I forced myself to go to Milwaukee—you do whatever it takes to find success, to make yourself successful. Life was looking up. Finally!

Chapter EIGHT

A Good Guy

The first step to getting the things you want out of life is this: Decide what you want.

—Ben Stein

There are a lot of things I can pull off because of my confidence in my character and personality. I can say things, be sarcastic, be a little sassy, whatever, and I can get away with it because it's part of my presentation—it's who I am. No apologies. No excuses. Someone else who lacks confidence or who's not as comfortable as I am can't quite say the same things and get away with it. They're going to come off a little jerky or worse, like a total bitch. The key is to know yourself. Live in your comfort zone. Confidence is a learned trait, but it requires practice. Like anything you want to get really good at, it takes time and practice.

Confidence is a big word in my life, a big part of who I am on the track and off. Confidence is what guides me through all of life's challenges. I know without a doubt that I am strong enough to get through anything life throws my way. I developed my confidence through years of creating a strong self-image as a means for survival. It all boils down to inner strength—having a belief structure that says, "This is how I want to live my life." For some people it's religion that guides those choices. For others it's a strong sense of self-worth or self-belief. Whatever gets you there—it's never too late to have unshakable confidence and a strong belief in yourself.

> **Given the opportunity, every human being has the same possibility for spiritual growth.**
> **—*Mohandas K. Gandhi***

When I was a little girl I had three wishes. The first was to race and win the Indy 500, the second was to meet Leonardo DiCaprio, and the third was to marry my then boyfriend Paul. I had one of those "magic" eight balls that I would shake and ask questions of all the time. "Will I race in the Indy 500?" "Will I win?" Various answers would appear through a small window at the bottom of the ball. The answers were "yes," "no," "maybe," "try again tomorrow," and so on. These days, I no longer need that magic eight ball to find answers to life's questions. I have put my faith in God. I trust that he has a bigger-picture plan for me. Knowing that there is a higher power that guides my life and the decisions I make for myself and my future has taken a huge burden off of me. It's comforting for me to know that there are lessons to be learned each and every day in the smallest things and the biggest disasters. As I said earlier, you can't just sit around and expect things to happen, but my faith has given me a brighter side to the tough times. I certainly believe that God led me to the great love of my life.

I realize that most people have some kind of belief system in their lives. Until 2005, when I began to learn about the Bible and became a Catholic, I hadn't put much credence in religion. I was raised in a home with no real religious beliefs, yet I always prayed, because I believed in God.

My parents taught me to make good decisions based on what I believed to be the right thing to do. If I had to think twice about something, it was probably wrong. That was the extent of my belief structure until I met Paul. I was twenty-one when I realized dating should be fun and that my failed relationships were not about what was wrong with me, but rather about my choice in men. If I had stayed in high school in Illinois, who knows, maybe I would have dated the captain of the football team, been named prom queen, and lived happily ever after. But that isn't the path I chose. I didn't have a normal teenage life. I grew up quickly, was more mature than most of the kids my age, had a penchant for slightly older guys, and had the freedom to make mistakes. Those errors in judgment taught me a lot. Most important, they taught me what I wanted in a relationship and proved to me what I could do without.

It wasn't until I became completely comfortable with myself that I recognized I had nothing but time and options. I had a full life ahead of me to date, mingle, and work hard at my job. It was only a short time after that epiphany that I met my future husband.

> **The first great step is to like yourself enough**
> **to pick someone who likes you, too.**
> **—Jane O'Reilly**

Meeting my husband, Paul, was nothing short of miraculous. We met in 2001 shortly after my return to the United States from England. I was about to start racing Formula Atlantic. I pulled a muscle in my hip doing yoga. I was trying to compete with the people on a television program at 6 o'clock in the morning, before my eyes were fully open, let alone my glutes! I had stressed the muscles in my right gluteus medius (the back upper part of my hip) so badly that I was unable to walk without a tremendous amount of pain. I certainly couldn't run or continue doing my yoga. I was in a lot of pain and was worried it would impact my driving. Finally, after limping for a month or so, I knew I had to see a doctor, and so did my boss, Bob, who was sick of hearing me complain about the constant pain.

I was in Phoenix to test Atlantic cars for the upcoming season. Bob Rahal suggested I go see his friend "Doogie," a nickname for Paul because, like the television character Doogie Howser, M.D., Paul is young and smart. Bob called and made the appointment for me to see Doogie when I was in Phoenix.

Paul ("Doogie") walked into the examination room, looked at my chart, looked up at me, and seemed a little confused. Apparently Bob had told Paul that one of his drivers, Danny, needed to come in and see him. Paul must have assumed that Danny was a guy, so when he saw me sitting in the exam room, imagine the surprised look on his face!

He was going to ask if my boyfriend was in the bathroom.

Now I am not sure how I would have reacted to that question. My gut tells me that if Paul had asked me that question, he would have been in the hole with me. I'm not sure I would have been as interested in him if he had asked me that question. Once I introduced myself, it all came together for him.

Paul ever the picture of a confident, cool, and collected professional, ended up treating me. I was totally unaware of his confusion until we talked about this misunderstanding for the first time in early 2005. We had a good laugh over the huge mistake that almost was because ours was the relationship that almost wasn't!

Paul's confidence caught my attention right away. I am attracted to people who have the same level of self-assurance that I do. We got along from the first moment he walked into the room. There was an instantly recognizable comfort between us. We are both a little sarcastic, and we playfully bantered throughout the examination.

After he finished my treatment, I casually asked if there was anyplace good to eat near his office?

He hadn't eaten, it was 8 o'clock in the evening, and I did not want to go back to the hotel to eat by myself. I thought it might be fun to get to know him a little better. Since Paul had stayed after his normal business hours and treated me as a favor to Bob, I thought it would be a kind gesture to take him to dinner. To my delight, Paul agreed to have dinner with me. We went for sushi and talked for hours. He suggested I come back in two days for another treatment and for a customized training program he would create for me. Two days later, I returned to see Dr. Doogie. OK, I'll admit that I tried to look cute that day. It must have worked because I asked Paul to dinner again that night, and he said yes.

We kept in touch for several months, talking on the phone and sending e-mail. As the holiday season approached, I sent Paul a Christmas card. It was a lighthearted card. I was careful not to seem too interested. Do you think writing in the card that "I feel another injury coming on. Thanks for the butt massage!" was too standoffish?

Not long after the holidays, I was in Los Angeles for business. Again I called Paul, and he flew to LA to meet me for dinner. For some strange reason, we found ourselves holding hands as we walked down the street. Up to this point, we had just forged a friendship. I remember feeling a little uncomfortable, unsure of what to think. I thought maybe this was just his way of being nice to me. I was gun shy. I didn't want to open myself up to be hurt. I hadn't had a lot of boyfriends—certainly none who had been as nice and polite as Paul. All of this was new and uncharted territory for me. Was Paul the "good guy" I had been searching for?

I found myself calling him whenever I was in the Phoenix area testing cars and practicing at Firebird Raceway in Chandler, Arizona, during the off-season winter months. Phoenix is a popular place for racers to go in the off-season because the weather is warm and predictable, as opposed to what it is in Columbus, Ohio, where I lived at the time. When I wasn't practicing, I found myself wanting to spend more and more time with Paul. Our occasional dinners were turning into regular occasions. I liked being around him. He's funny, he's brilliant, he's sexy, and he makes me feel good. He is the only man I ever dated who opens doors for me. I once told Paul he didn't need to open my door. He replied, "I'll open your door forever."

Forever?

There's a thought . . . what did that mean?

Forever?

I don't think either of us knew what was happening, but I'm certain we were both grateful for it.

The more time we spent together, the more time I wanted to spend together. Paul was working a lot with professional baseball teams for spring training. I was supposed to go back to Columbus from Phoenix for two days and then head back to Phoenix again for a photo shoot for my primary sponsor, Argent. Paul suggested I stay in his guesthouse for the weekend, thinking it would be more comfortable and might give me a much-needed sense of home. He explained that since he was working so much it was no imposition. I thought about it and decided it might be a good idea. I weighed the 85 degree weather in Phoenix against the sub-zero winter weather back home. It was an easy choice. Hello, Phoenix!

When Paul was around, we went hiking together, went to movies, and began what has become the relationship for the rest of my life. I was not sick of this guy, and I always got sick of the guys I dated. I now understand that none of those guys were the "right" ones. As my relationship with Paul evolved, I couldn't have been happier.

In the spring of 2004, Paul and I were together on Easter. It was my first purposeful trip to see him. Prior to this, most of my trips were still for the good weather. I had never put so much effort into dating someone before I met Paul. I once mentioned to Paul that I was a pretty good cook—and most of the time I am. I wanted to make a meal to show him how good I was. I wanted to make a meal he'd never forget!

Boy, did I ever. I made scallops. I've never been known for being shy, and when it comes to seasoning my food, I'm no exception. I put a little too much red pepper on the scallops. We ate them, but they were so hot that we drank our wine like it was water. I was worried he might not want to go out with me after that because I had made such a lousy meal. But we stuck it out together . . . bad meal that it was. After the great bottle of wine and spending Easter together like an old married couple, I wrote, ". . . just like an old married couple, and I loved it!" on the cork from the bottle of wine. Somehow I knew I wanted to commemorate this moment. That cork sits on our drink bar today.

> **Love doesn't make the world go 'round. Love is what makes the ride worthwhile.**
> **—*Franklin P. Jones***

A week later I was racing in Long Beach, California. Despite my lousy cooking, Paul came out to the race. From that weekend on, we were committed to each other. We spent so much time together. I never got bored being with him. I knew something special was happening, but I didn't want to think about it. Things were great. I was happy. For the first time in my life, I let the relationship unfold and present itself for whatever it was or would become. I was so grateful to be in it.

I love that Paul is an independent thinker, that he has a mind of his own. He constantly challenges me to be a better person. He has raised the bar in terms of expectations for what I can achieve. He has taught me tolerance, patience, the value of being nicer, softer, and thinking globally, seeing things in the big picture instead of just thinking about myself. We have given each other the gift of unconditional love and unwavering support.

For the first time in my life, I have someone else to think about when making decisions. I have another person whose life is affected by my actions. It's a new level of responsibility—one that I fully embrace. We complement each other in ways I could never have imagined. Our energy balances each of our lives. He is the yin to my yang. For all of my aggressive, "out there," in-your-face ways, Paul is soft-spoken, calm, and thoughtful. I see things as black and white; Paul can see the gray. I like to shop and spend money; Paul thinks of ways to make or save it! Our friendship continues to grow, and the depth of our love has become infinite.

Love is a fruit in season at all times, and within the reach of every hand.

—Mother Teresa

Love—a word that is overused, underused, misused, abused, and misunderstood. If you love, whether it's a person or a sport or an idea or belief, love is really all you need in life. It's more powerful than anything I have ever known. Pure love. If you truly love, you are willing to go through whatever it takes to nurture that love. You're willing to work through anything because your love is far more powerful than the problem or challenge that stands in your way. I find this to be true for my love for Paul, but also for my love of racing.

Maintaining a long-distance relationship with Paul took a lot of will and want. It required a desire to grow the relationship in ways I had never known before he and I met. All I needed in my life was to love Paul, and I was willing to go anywhere, fly anywhere at any time to nurture that love. I was open to receiving love, and I loved it!

I never thought of myself as a romantic person. I was never the kind of woman who liked getting flowers or having doors opened for me. But Paul showed me that it's OK to be romantic—to be romanced and to be romantic. I slipped into my role as his girlfriend like I slip into a pair of Manolo Blahniks or the cockpit of my car. It's a perfect fit.

Racing has become a part of Paul's life, but it is not the focus of our life off the track. We both love to travel and plan to take every opportunity during my off-season to see and experience different cultures and discover unimaginable corners of the globe, with one condition—he gets to drive! Yeah, it's kind of a well-known fact that racecar drivers generally make their spouses a little nervous when it comes to regular, everyday driving. Our general rule is that neither of us gets to comment on the other's driving if we offer the keys but the other declines. So I can't lean over and glance at the speedometer and mention he's going the speed limit, and he's not allowed to grab onto the dashboard and cringe at my incessant tailgating! It's an agreement that helps make our relationship work.

From the outside looking in, I don't think anyone would have thought that I was at a place in my life where I could possibly think of settling down. I live a life that literally moves at 220 mph. I am a busy woman. I have a full-time career. I have sponsor commitments and commercial endorsements. I have people pulling at me from every direction twenty-four hours a day, seven days a week, and yet I found time and room in my life to make my relationship with Paul a priority. I have always believed the right person can make your life better, just as the wrong person can make your life worse.

When I met Paul, I was a little apprehensive about pursuing a serious relationship for fear of what the impact might be on my career. I wasn't sure how he would be perceived around the racetrack—whether my team would see him as a distraction. But I cared for him so much, more than anyone I had ever been interested in before. Paul is a "take care of himself" kind of guy, so he made the transition easy.

There is a seventeen-year age difference between Paul and me. At first glance, it might seem that our age difference would bring a set of challenges to our relationship. I know my father was always concerned that I not let my personal life derail my professional life. My past history with men was to choose the "bad boy" type, and until I met Paul, my parents were not terribly happy with my choices in some men. But it didn't take them long to recognize that Paul was a very different kind of man, one I could easily embrace—and I do as often as I can! He's mature, smart, settled in his life, and successful in his career, and he has the qualities my parents would have hoped for when it came time for their little girl to settle down. After the first time they met, my dad told me that Paul is perfect for me. Yes! Perfect.

Paul's presence added to my race experience. It became a good thing, as I found myself calmer and more relaxed before a race, and comfort in his arms after—literally. He offered me strong moral support and tremendous wisdom from his heart and soul. And let's face it, he's a damn good massage therapist, so it didn't hurt to have him trackside whenever I needed him!

Paul proposed to me on Thanksgiving 2004, which we spent with my family in Illinois. As much as I knew we would someday get married, I have to admit that he caught me a bit off guard with the proposal. Early Thanksgiving morning, as the sun came up, we woke up too. Paul got out of bed for a minute, went to the bathroom, and came back to snuggle for a few minutes. He popped up again and got out of bed for a second time. I looked at him, wondering what he was doing. "Are you going to the bathroom again?"

He couldn't say what he was really doing, so he said nothing at all. Before I knew what was happening, he got down on one knee, and quickly grabbed the ring that was hidden under my side of the mattress.

"Will you marry me forever?"

I didn't even see the ring at first. I was too excited about the proposal to see the ring. I laughed and cried and giggled and laughed and cried and grabbed his head and pulled it into my chest and held him tight as I cried.

I was completely shocked.

It was perfect.

But I hadn't answered.

Paul asked, "Well?"

I said, *"Yes! Yes! Yes!"*

And that's when I saw my beautiful engagement ring. I let out a loud, *"Wow!"*

I held my hand out so he could gently slide the ring onto my finger. I was officially engaged.

Every girl wants to be surprised with a proposal. Who wants to wait around wondering, "When is it going to happen? Will it be today?"

My father and sister both knew Paul was going to propose. Of course, Paul had asked my father for permission to marry me. And he had enlisted my sister's advice on whether or not I would say yes. My mom was totally as shocked as I was. She had no clue. I walked . . . OK, I ran downstairs, hiding my hands behind my back. Mom was wondering what I was doing? What was I hiding? I slammed my hands down on the kitchen table, revealing my shiny new diamond engagement ring!

"Oh my God! Is that real?"

That's all Paul heard, as he was still upstairs, brushing his teeth. He looked in the mirror and said out loud, "What else do I have to do?"

And in case you're wondering about those three wishes I had as a little girl?

Two out of three ain't bad. Meeting Leo isn't the priority it used to be!

Love is all you need.

—John Lennon

Chapter NINE

Embrace the Difference

Real confidence comes from knowing and accepting yourself—your strengths and your limitations—in contrast to depending on affirmation from others.

—Judith M. Bardwick

A woman living in a man's world has been a recurring theme throughout my life. Having to prove myself over and over has become a part of my everyday living. It took me some time to understand and accept that there are benefits to being different. Once I did,

Danica Patrick

I wanted to do everything I could to embrace it and capitalize on what made me special.

As much as I wanted to fit in, and as hard as I tried to be respected, I never seemed to penetrate that wall of male bonding or find acceptance from my peers. Even when I deserved to be commended or congratulated, I was never given the adulation I earned simply because I was a girl—which made me different, and in that respect kept me on the outside of the world of the men. Those years allowed me to focus on taking my differences and using them as an advantage. They helped me to find a sense of security within myself, because I was definitely not going to receive any kind of support from the outside.

Think about what kind of world this would be if we were all the same? If we all had the same things to offer, there would be no appreciation for the balance in the universe. Without bad days, you can't appreciate the good. Without defeat, you can't appreciate victory. Everybody has something they are really good at. You certainly have skills you can do as well as if not better than anyone else. There is something in your body, your mind, or your spirit that sets you apart, that makes you different from the rest of the world. I was fortunate enough to find my something "different" when I was ten years old. Of course, I realize that doesn't happen for everyone, and that in itself is something that makes me different, because it happened to me.

Courage is fear that has said its prayers.
—Karl Barth

Win with Confidence

There have been many times in my life when my attitude and level of self-assurance was the difference between winning and losing. Even when I don't win a race, I see victory in how I handle my losses or what I learned from the experience. Confidence and self-belief are like muscles that have to be built and used to be strong. My confidence has helped me to make smart choices and to keep cool along the way so that I never veered off course from my dream of becoming a professional driver. My courage keeps me driving with or without my confidence. There were a lot of opportunities for me to waver from the center of the road, but I had a bigger plan, a bigger strength, and that knowledge led me to never fall into situations of peer pressure or make choices that would ruin my career. The risk/reward ratio just never made sense in my life.

It's been said that "ability without ambition is like kindling wood without a spark." Ambition is not a negative trait. It is an essential element to achieve success on any level. Any woman who becomes a leader in her workplace deals with the same kind of issues I face as the only woman competing for a win on the track. Jealousy, distrust, lack of approval from peers, doubt, and the constant need to demonstrate that you've earned your place in the company—they're all good excuses that work for a while, but if you're good at what you do, you'll make it.

Everybody is entitled to their own opinion. In the end their opinions don't mean a thing if your performance is superior. Those who talk negatively about other people are usually jealous, angry, threatened people. I've dealt with a lot of people questioning my performance as a driver—everyone from other team owners, drivers, journalists, and racing aficionados. I've been called dangerous, erratic, aggressive, and out of control. You know what? I don't care.

Racing is not about being masculine or feminine. It's about being a damn good driver. The track doesn't discriminate. Man or woman, you either have the skill or you don't. I find it's best to leave politics to the politicians. There's simply no room for excessive bullshit when your job is driving a racecar. If I and my team, my pit crew, my engineer, my agent, my manager, or my sponsors are not all sharing the same goal, we are not working toward the same outcome, which, for me, is winning races. If we're not working with one another, then we are working against each other. That surely defeats the purpose of all being in business together. That lack of productivity means we are not winning races or living up to the obligations we all share as business associates. In any work environment, that has an impact of immeasurable proportion.

> **Winning is important to me, but what brings me real joy is the experience of being fully engaged in whatever I'm doing.**
> —*Phil Jackson*

I've learned that I don't need to be friends with the other drivers to compete, but I definitely want their acceptance and respect on the track. You get that only by earning it. It's not an automatic thing. If earning their respect makes me work harder, then I'm the one who reaps all the benefits. Telling myself I don't care about what other people think is one of the ways I have built my self-confidence over the years.

Tell yourself something long enough and sooner or later you'll start to believe it. Think of all of the ways your life will benefit by believing it doesn't matter what other people think. Confidence comes from within. It allows you to be comfortable and hold your head up in any situation. It's proving yourself over and over and over again, every time you face your toughest competition.

Confidence is when other people worry that you're in the game. It's walking right up to someone—anyone—shaking his hand hard, looking him right in the eyes, and talking to him face to face.

It's asking questions others wouldn't dare.

It's putting on a brave face even when you know there's a shadow of doubt or, for me, when I get nervous "butterfly" feelings in my stomach at the beginning of every race.

Everybody wants someone working for them with moxie, with confidence and courage. Confidence is expressive, but it should never be confused with being arrogant. It's shown by making eye contact with people when you talk to them. There's something about intense eye contact that gives you a connection with someone, if only for that moment. It lets him know you are present and care about what he is saying. It can convey that you are angry, attracted, joyful, sad, or aware.

A long time ago, I decided to never wear sunglasses when I am meeting someone for the first time. It's impersonal. My dad taught me to have a firm handshake—to "shake like you mean it." People have written about my handshake and how hard it is. I have made it a point to never let someone say I shake like a girl. I can look confident, feel confident, and be confident without ever saying a single word. It's a presence.

When I'm at the track I get a look of intense focus on my face. I call it my race face. I get a bit of a frown face on, and my eyes become squinty. People sometimes mistake this expression for being mad or upset—it is neither. I would rather look that way than any other way. Looking intense and focused is never wrong, and it can never be confused with looking arrogant, cocky, or over-confident.

Figuring out what makes you different in this world is one of the best ways to tap into your inner strengths. Find out what you're good at. If you're a fiery-tempered person, how can you use your aggression in a positive way? You surely won't be happy working in the local public library, but maybe you can tap that aggression and become a boxing coach or a salesperson? If you are an impatient person, waiting tables probably isn't your calling, but a job with instant gratification, like cutting hair, might be perfect for you. Try to use your differences to your advantage by putting yourself in situations that are beneficial to your skill set.

Destiny is not a matter of chance; it is a matter of choice. It is not a thing to be waited for; it is a thing to achieve.

—William Jennings Bryan

My husband and I love to use the word "embrace" when we are dealing with each other's eccentricities. We started using the phrase "Just embrace it" pretty early on in our relationship, and we've found that instead of allowing those things to become irritating habits, "embracing" them has helped us form an appreciation for the little things that make us different. For example, when I am in a restaurant, I order my food in a very specific way. My friends think I'm like Meg Ryan's character in *When Harry Met Sally* because I am very detailed about how I want my food prepared and served. At the end of the day, it's my food, and I like to eat my food exactly the way I want it. I usually start my order by apologizing in advance to the server, but then I get right down to business asking:

"How is the chicken prepared?"

"Is the chicken grilled or sautéed?"

"Can I have it plain, without any seasoning?"

"I want my salad with no dressing and no sauces on anything."

At first Paul thought I was being a little too picky, too demanding. Every time he'd give me a disapproving look, I'd respond by saying, "Just embrace it."

One day he came to me and said, "You know what? It has made a huge difference in my patience for your quirks. After you told me to 'embrace it,' I realized all you were really saying to me is this is who you are. It's just you, and I love you for every part of who you are."

Ever since, whenever something comes up that's a little odd, quirky, or different, we look at each other and simply say, "Just embrace it!" In the big picture, whatever that moment is, it's just a moment, and that moment will pass. Five minutes, ten seconds, one day, or one month—they're all just moments in time. Just embrace that time, regardless of the circumstances; take a deep breath and say, "This too shall pass."

Perhaps, if you're lucky, you might learn something from it. You might see things from a new perspective or from someone else's point of view. And regardless of whether or not you agree, having an open mind is always a good thing, even if it doesn't always feel that way at the time.

There were times when I hid being different, at least to the extent that I could. When I was in England, I deliberately lived like one of the guys in order to get along and to fit in. It was the only way I thought I could get through that painful and difficult phase of my life. I literally protected myself from being too girly. I was careful not to be too appealing or too feminine. I was closing myself off from being misunderstood or judged for wanting to be a racecar driver.

Running away from who I was meant I was living my life in a constant state of turmoil. Denying who you are or hiding behind some façade becomes like a cancer in your body that just spreads. Eventually it will manifest itself and take a toll on every aspect of your life. Living an inauthentic life holds you back from achieving your full potential.

It wasn't until I did a photo shoot for *FHM* magazine in 2002 that I had a full understanding that being a girl in a man's world wasn't a negative thing. That shoot changed a lot of people's perception of me—including my own. I thought it was pretty cool when I was asked to do a spread in their annual "Speed" section, a twenty-page layout dedicated to hot cars . . . and, I guess, me. I knew *FHM* wasn't putting a girl in the magazine who couldn't sell magazines or who didn't look pretty.

I had no idea what I would wear—a swimsuit, a race suit, or something totally different. I was tremendously flattered to be asked. It validated me in a way I had never known. Up to that point, every article I did, every magazine shoot, newspaper story, and television appearance focused on racing. *FHM* was different. It focused on my sexuality. For the first time in my life, I felt sexy, feminine, tough, and attractive all at the same time.

I worked hard at looking good in those photos. I worked out like a maniac and was so strict with my food. Let's just say that, like everything else I do, I took this experience to the limit. I tried to tell myself that they wouldn't have to retouch a thing (they did—magazines retouch practically every photo you see). I no longer had a desire to hide being a woman from the world. In fact, I wanted to show it off—and I did—in every way, front, back, sitting, lying down. It was great fun.

That spread forever eradicated having to answer for being "the girl" in racing, but it brought a whole new set of questions. Reporters went nuts wanting to know if I used my femininity to advance my career? How did I feel about becoming a sex symbol? It was crazy at first, but not long after the magazine was published I had an epiphany.

Why not?

Why not use whatever assets I have?

I'm confident in myself as a driver.

It's obvious I'm a girl, so why not use it as a tool?

There are benefits to it—benefits that I simply can't deny. People will doubt you, make you prove yourself over and over again, unlike a man might have to do. So what?

Here's the upshot. Sponsors such as Honda, Peak Antifreeze, and Secret deodorant have stepped up and are using a sexy woman racecar driver as a unique marketing tool. Let's face it, guys don't sell antifreeze quite the same way I do.

Danica Patrick

Everybody has assets they bring to any given situation. Learning to use them—better yet, learning not to be afraid to use them—is incredibly emancipating. It's taken me a long time, but I now know, without a doubt, that it's good to be a girl!

Though I wouldn't do it again, *FHM* gave people something to talk about. For the first time, people saw Danica Patrick as a woman first and a racer second. I had never known that kind of attention, and to be honest, it made me a little uncomfortable. I wouldn't change a thing about that experience. Because of it, I no longer need a sexy photo shoot to prove to the world that I'm a sexy woman. So if you're listening, Anna Wintour, I am ready for *Vogue!*

That shoot helped me overcome my fears of others perceiving me as being too girly or out of place in the racing world. It helped me get sponsors because it generated a lot of attention. It was a risky decision on my part, but deep down I know the heightened awareness was a benefit. It got people talking. They are still talking and still running those photos. So was it worth it? You bet!

Self-respect is to the soul as oxygen is to the body. Deprive a person of oxygen, and you kill his body; deprive him of self-respect, and you kill his spirit.

—Thomas Szasz

Being a girl is who I am, and that photo shoot opened the door for me to just be myself. As my confidence grew, so did my self-acceptance.

Ultimately, I have learned that you've got to rock what you've got, whatever that is.

One of the benefits of being the only girl racing in the various series I have participated in is that I get to spend a lot of time around men, which has given me unusual perspective and insight into the way guys think. Women tend to over-rationalize, whereas men are very simple and obvious. No one edits themselves when I'm around, that's for sure. It's not like they curtail their conversations because there's a woman present. I hear firsthand what a guy is thinking when a pretty girl in a short skirt and high heels walks by. There were times in England when I found myself checking girls out with the guys, just to fit in. I'd ask, "Did you see that girl? She was hot!"

I think I have a pretty good understanding of the male psyche today as a result of my time spent being one of the boys. I think it has helped me in my relationship with Paul. Most women spend a lot of time trying to figure out what their husbands or boyfriends are really thinking. I suppose I have the luxury of having spent so much time around men that I get it in a way most women simply can't. Come on, ladies . . . it's usually the most obvious answer, or they're just hungry!

I have wondered what it might be like if my husband were a professional racecar driver and someone I had to compete against. He's a very passionate guy, and he loves to win as much as I do. I'm guessing we'd be fierce competitors. Like me, Paul never quits. If he's competing, he wants to be the best. Since we share those qualities, we sometimes face each other in areas in which we both know we excel, yet one of us is slightly better than the other. Paul is such a good athlete; there's not much he can't do and do well. However, when it comes to yoga . . . well, let's just say I'm the one leading the class.

Danica Patrick

We try not to get into serious competition with each other because I know we're both very aware that we are serious competitors, and we could run with it to the point of creating unnecessary tension. So instead of trying to outdo each other, we have committed to accompanying each other. Whether it's cooking, running, hiking, or any other activity we do together, we try to complement each other and to work together on everything.

In any relationship, be it personal or professional, sharing the same goal and making the same commitment is the key to success. All relationships are never-ending learning experiences. Even relationships that don't work out teach us something of value. For me, my relationships prior to meeting my husband taught me various things I didn't want in a partner, Paul is the first man I have been with that I've had total confidence in knowing we are both in this relationship forever—and that I have his whole heart and he has mine. Our priorities are the same, and our commitment to live up to those priorities is unshakable.

When you know something is right, nothing and no one can tell you it's wrong. Paul tried to talk himself out of our relationship in the beginning. He thought I was too young, too immature, that I needed to experience more things in life before settling down. Actually, I think the fact that my career was just beginning to become high profile worried him in terms of how he might handle the temptations of fame. He's a private person and a professional who doesn't need the spotlight, but he was willing to stand by me for the right reasons. The more he tried to convince himself that this was wrong, the more he became convinced that it was right. He had a harder time justifying letting go than he did holding on.

Our differences make our relationship everything wonderful that it is. Instead of rejecting those things that make us vastly different as people, we choose to embrace them and have built a loving, trusting partnership in the process.

OK, so I've spent a lot of time telling you how wonderful things are in my relationship, but by now you must be thinking, "C'mon, Danica. It can't all be sunshine and roses."

What relationship is?

I'm known to have something of a temper. Of course, Paul and I have discussions and disagreements. They usually start over something stupid, like me forgetting to write down the number of outlets for the contractor or spending too much money on shoes and purses. Whatever it is that starts our fights is usually just the catalyst for us to talk about a bigger issue that is brewing.

Before we began dating, Paul was never a "talker." He was the kind of guy who kept his feelings inside. I, on the other hand, come from a family of brutally honest communicators. I spent my youth traveling in the car with my family, often for twenty hours at a time as we went from race to race. If something was wrong, if I was upset, if my sister was mad, whatever the situation, we talked about it because there was nothing worse than sitting in that car angry and in silence. I was taught to be honest with my feelings from a very early age. Whatever you have to say, just go for it, because until you do, it'll just simmer until it reaches a boiling point, and that's never good for anyone. Holding things in is a really poor option. Regardless of what the issue was, my family and I worked through it, fast and furious.

Paul is nonconfrontational, whereas I am all about confrontation. Needless to say, our different approaches to communication took some getting used to. I was persistent about us talking to each other, especially in the beginning of our relationship. And though it took him a while to embrace where I was coming from, he has come around and has gotten very good at opening up and talking to me about anything and everything. It's a big part of what makes our relationship work. We don't give each other the space to let our minds run wild, to wonder what is going on.

We've all been there. We can't get our guy on the phone, and for some reason we conjure up thoughts that he must be out cheating with another woman. It's ridiculous, but we've all done it. Getting rid of conflict right away helps avoid those worst-case-scenario thought patterns. Who has time to pretend anyway? It all goes back to living authentically.

If you're angry with someone, be angry—but tell that person, and work through it. I've never been afraid to speak my mind, and my brutal, unfiltered honesty has become something I've become known for. I've never been a girl who adheres to convention or shies away from controversy or conflict. On the contrary, I have a strong belief in thinking outside the box and putting myself out there in ways that other people may view as being aggressive. Without those traits, I could never be doing what I do. I wouldn't be setting records or shattering images of what a girl—or anyone, for that matter—can achieve if she puts her mind to it.

I've never tried to be something that I'm not. I've just lived my life in a way in which I am frank, honest, and true to myself. In doing that, I don't have to change a thing about myself or the way I live. I don't have to do anything extra because I am out there giving a 100 percent

On our way for a run thirty
minutes after Paul asked
me to marry him.
Bev Patrick

All dressed up for
Thanksgiving 2005.

Paul and I on our way to
dinner. Does his hand
make my butt look small?

"It'll be OK, honey." He survived.

Girls' night out on Thursday before my wedding day. From left to right: Kim, Amber, me, Marni, Meredith, Shondra, Tina, Mary Ann, and Brooke.
Bev Patrick

Paul and I at our rehearsal dinner the night before our wedding.

Brooke and I dancing my wedding night away.

Rock what you've got.

My bridal party. From left to right: my sister, Brooke, and my best friends Heather, Mary Ann, and Marni, looking beautiful on my big day.
Alan Mermelstein

Mom and I trying not to smudge our lipstick.
Alan Mermelstein

I knew this would happen. Tears of joy on my wedding day.
Alan Mermelstein

Our first photo as Mr. and Mrs. Hospenthal.
Alan Mermelstein

Presidents of the fan clubs! Tony Kanaan and me at the 2005 Indy 500.

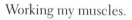

Working my muscles.

The two most important men in my life getting ready to experience Indy firsthand . . . but at only 180 mph!

Keeping the mood light during a long month at Indy. From left to right: Dad, Brooke, Mom, and me.

Indy 500 drivers meeting. Race face on!

Brian Spurlock

Brian Spurlock

God, keep me safe.
Praying with Paul and
IRL chaplain Bob Hills.

Getting ready to qualify for the Indy 500. Cold
day, cold tires. At least I saved it in turn one.

Green flag at the 2005 Indy 500. Here I come!
Brian Spurlock

Leader of the pack. All the boys chasing me at 230 mph during the 2005 Indy.
Paul Webb

Check out the leader board . . . I'm number 16 . . . first place!

The picture says it all. Dad and me moments after the 2005 Indy 500.

Paul Webb

Good days still hurt sometimes. Walking to my press conference after the Indy 500.

I prefer red wine, but spraying champagne is much more fun.
Paul Webb

My piece of debris is in the Indianapolis Motor Speedway Hall of Fame. Dad was proud.
Paul Webb

Where were we a year before this, Bob? Bob Rahal and I fielding the media after a race.
Paul Webb

Danica mania

Brian Spurlock

Paul Webb

Brian Spurlock

Brian Spurlock

Danica! Can I Be Your... Physical Therapist? Class of 2008

effort each and every day. I just keep truckin' on, the same way I always have, because it works for me.

A Bigger Responsibility

There's a responsibility that comes with being a public personality. I have an obligation to live my life in way that leads by example. I never gave much thought to the public part of being a racecar driver, but when I see young kids at a track wearing a T-shirt with my name on it or standing in line for an autograph at a race, I realize my life has influenced theirs. Recognizing that has helped me want to be a better role model to them.

I never had heroes growing up, just great role models. My parents were my best role models, giving me a strong set of values and teaching me to live responsibly. That knowledge has carried over into my adult life. I find myself having to make decisions about what I will endorse (watches, clothing, sunglasses) or won't (anything I don't believe in) or which photo shoots I will agree to (*Sports Illustrated*) and ones that I won't (*Playboy*.) I have to factor in that I have a young fan base that looks up to me. It's a responsibility I am so flattered to have. It really humbles me. I'm so grateful for the opportunity to be a woman raising the bar for other girls—future champions coming up behind me, whether they are drivers, politicians, doctors, teachers, whatever they dream they can be. My presence in racing is making a difference. It is bringing on change. It is growing the sport and making people aware of the league.

I may not have been the first woman to race in the Indy 500, but it's a comfort to know that, because of all the women before me, I surely won't be the last.

All that makes me different in my life has made me unique and afforded me a tremendous opportunity to effect change. So the next time someone points out something about you that makes you feel different, that makes you feel like an outsider, you tell them that all of those things are what makes you great—that being different means you're not like them—and that's all good.

Chapter TEN

What a Ride! Racing the Indy 500

Lady and gentlemen, start your engines!

Mari Hulman George, Indianapolis Motor Speedway Chairman, announcing the start of the 2005 Indy 500

In racing terms, the word "ride" has a lot of different meanings. A ride is often how a racer refers to her team. It can also describe the experience of getting behind the wheel of a racecar. The greatest moment in my career so far was racing my first Indy 500. While there have been other women who have made it to the "Brickyard" (as the famous Indianapolis Motor Speedway is often called), I became the first woman to ever lead a lap in the world's most famous race. I led for a total of nineteen exhilarating laps, doing what I could to hold off the charge of Dan Wheldon, Vitor Meira, and Bryan Herta, with just eight laps remaining in the 200-lap classic. What a ride!

The Indy 500 was my fifth IRL Series race. I knew I didn't have the experience that the other drivers had and there were still a lot of things for me to learn. The thrill of racing in this huge event was enormous for me on every level. It represented the culmination of all my sweat and perseverance, training for fourteen years to compete with the best of the best in open-wheel racing. It is truly a dream come true, a dream I've dreamed for fourteen years.

Racing in the Indy 500 is the equivalent of being nominated for an Oscar, playing in the Super Bowl, or finding yourself on center court, playing the finals at Wimbledon. Winning the Indy 500 is like taking home the award for Best Actress, wearing the championship ring, or raising the silver cup in victory in front of a cheering crowd.

> **Don't get mad; don't get even; get ahead.**
> —*Chris Matthews*

When I was a kid, watching the Indy 500 was a Patrick family tradition. It meant Sundays on the couch with my mom, dad, and sister, eating chips and dip, falling asleep after thirty minutes and waking up just in time to see the very end. It's always been a part of my past—and now it was an imminent part of my future and racing history.

Racing in the 2005 Indianapolis 500 would be a life-altering experience for me and a history-making and record-setting race for the IRL. This was the event in which I would prove that behind the wheel, everything is equal for a man and a woman. My car has no idea if I am male or female. I'm just another driver on the track, and it makes no difference who is behind the wheel. A driver has to perform. Racing is about results. To be successful and accomplish what I want to accomplish, I had to be successful. I had a lot of people backing me who believed in me, but most important, I believed in myself.

> **Never explain what you're doing. This wastes a good deal of time, and rarely gets through. Show them through your action; if they don't understand it, **** 'em, maybe you'll hook them with the next action.**
>
> **—Abbie Hoffman**

Racing at Indianapolis is a month-long event involving three weeks of practice that lead up to the big event—the Indy 500. I knew I would be the only woman racing, but I was not thinking of myself as a woman driver, just another IndyCar driver out there to win. I have always raced against the guys. When we are sitting behind the wheel, we're all the same.

Sure, I had less experience than a lot of the drivers, but I also had last year's winning team behind me. I thought that was a big advantage going into the month. I have to give a lot of credit to my teammates Buddy Rice and Vitor Meira, because the setup for my car was somewhat built on what they ran at Indy the year before.

Coming to Indianapolis to race for the first time is exciting, but as a young driver I had to get past all of that initial anxiety and move toward doing what I came here for—to win. I had to approach the on-track issues like I would at any other race and get down to business.

As practice sessions commenced in early May, my speed and lap times continued to increase. I ran a day-high seventy-seven laps on Monday afternoon and topped my fast lap from Sunday by more than 1 mile an hour, which is significant in racing terms. In fact, my top speed of 222.741 mph surpassed the pole-winning speed 222.024 mph of last year's Indy 500 winner. Things were looking pretty good for a successful month. I had a lot of confidence I would qualify. For most people, that alone would have been the fulfillment of a dream. Not for me.

My team continued to slowly trim out the car with the hope of finding some more speed for me. I was practicing well and wanted to get better, go faster, and become stronger. It's easy to get caught up in practice times, but a lot of people were getting tows (drafting) during practice, which inflated their speeds, making it a little deceptive when it came to fastest time on the track. We continued to work our way through what we needed to be done as a team so I would be well prepared for Pole Day. Pole Day is a qualifying race, but at Indy it is the only day you can win the pole. The rest of the days are to fill the field of drivers for race day.

Much to my dismay, in 2005 Pole Day at the Indianapolis Motor Speedway was rained out! First-day qualifying was rescheduled for the next day, Sunday, May 15. I was headed into qualifying with the second-fastest lap of the month. It was hugely disappointing not to get out there after a week of practice. Our team was eager to make our qualifying run, but the weather didn't cooperate, so we had to wait another day. I was feeling very confident with my car's setup. Qualifying always seems to be a little different than practice because it's do-or-die time. I always get more nervous when I think I have a pole car—and I did. Thankfully, I would only have to wait one more night before I could have my first chance to qualify for Indy.

Pole Day—Sunday, May 15, 2005

I posted the fastest single lap on the first day of qualifying at 227.860 mph, but despite my speed, it was my first lap everyone was talking about. I nearly spun my car after taking the green flag to start my qualifying run. In my mind, I wanted to walk away from qualifying knowing that I left nothing on the table as far as speed. With that, when the green flag dropped, I never lifted my foot off the pedal until I knew I wouldn't get around the corner unless I did. The rear end of the car came around, I caught it; it came around again, I caught it, and that left me with a first lap average speed of 224.920 mph, much slower than expected but much faster than ending up in the wall, which I almost did. I quickly recovered to post a four-lap qualifying average of 227.004 mph, My time officially topped the sixth-place start of Lyn St. James in 1994. I now held the mark for the highest start for a female driver at Indianapolis—something to be proud of, but I left the track angry because I should have earned the pole. That was one of those situations where the only way I could feel better about the result was to find the bright side. Perhaps if I had qualified first, I would have been so busy and distracted by the pressure and obligations off the track that my race would have suffered. That's what I told myself to get through. In retrospect, I'm not sure there would have been any more pressure or one more minute to give to the media, but at the time, I somehow justified my fourth-place start as being better over the long haul.

Despite my time, I was disappointed because I had a car capable of winning the pole and I didn't succeed. If I could have run something close to my last three laps on my first, I would have surely won the pole. I was able to make up a lot of ground, but when I was more than 2 mph off, I had a lot of catching up to do. It was frustrating because I really wanted to be on the pole. My personal expectations had really increased since the start of the season, when I was qualifying fifteenth or worse.

I had officially qualified for the race, so the rest of my month here at Indy was all about getting ready for race day. We concentrated on running full fuel tanks and practiced running the car in traffic, something I needed more experience with for sure. All of my runs were aimed at learning how the car reacted in traffic. As I approached my final practice days, it was all about keeping the car in one piece and making sure it ran. My team guided me through my first experience at Indy, and I felt ready for the race.

Race day was approaching. It was Friday before the race, and the atmosphere was getting serious. I'd been here all month ramping up for this. Coming into the Indy 500, I had generated a lot of media buzz. There was an inordinate amount of attention on me, both as a professional driver and as a woman racing against the big boys of the IRL. The novelty of a female driver with a real shot at winning the Indy 500 attracted worldwide attention. I always knew I was a fast driver, so it was time to capitalize on that. I knew the media would come around.

My schedule off the track had become more grueling than the time I spent on the track practicing and qualifying for this month-long event. I wanted to do as much media as I could because I wanted the IRL series to grow and become a household name for fans. I began to realize that the outside commitments were taking an emotional and physical toll. There's nothing I could really do about it. I tried to ignore the mania that was building. After an exhausting week of nonstop press and media interviews and appearances, it was time to focus on the task at hand—winning. This was everything I had worked for—the pinnacle of success for an IRL driver. I had my sights set on going into the big race to win. If I'm out there doing something, I'm out there to win. I feel that I can beat everyone; I feel that I can win. What's the point of putting yourself through a tiresome, grueling, four-hour race if you're not on the track to taste victory?

I needed to relax as much as I could. I didn't want to over-commit and lose focus on why I was there. Being with my family helped me to stay calm and focused in what would otherwise have been an uncontrollable tide of attention. Race day was coming. Race day was coming. This was why I was at Indy.

Danica Patrick

Race Day, May 28, 2005

Despite my inexperience, I had trained for this day my whole life. I wanted to be extra-organized on this particular race morning. All of the ingredients were in place. I had top-notch equipment, the full backing of a winning team, and the talent and determination to make the most of my opportunity. On race day, my preparation is as much about what I don't do as it is about what I do. I was systematically reviewing my strategy in my mind. I needed a good driving strategy, good pit stops, a team with a clear idea of what needed to happen out there, and someone in my ear to keep me calm. OK, cool, I had all of that. Though I didn't have the same experience as the other drivers, I went into the race with the fastest overall lap time of the month, clocking in at 229.880 mph. A racer needs to be mindful of so many things at the start of a race. I didn't want to over-complicate things in my head. I spent the morning visualizing myself on the track—mentally taking every turn over and over in my head. I saw myself crossing the finish line, the checkered flag waving me through. I was beginning to build the rhythm of the race, keeping in mind the start, when the race gets under way, coming into the pit, and all of the potential mishaps inside the car. Could a rookie win the Indy 500? It was entirely possible. If I caught the right breaks, didn't make any mistakes, and had the racing gods smiling down on me, it was more than possible.

It took a lot of tweaking to get the car just right for race day; my engineer made adjustments along the way until he finally felt it was just right. With the advent of computer technology, I am among a new breed of racers who could easily overdose on the massive amounts of information my engineer has access to. I am not an information junkie. I have no need to know the specifics of what the computer indicates as problematic. I do review engineering data, which tell me everything that happened to my racecar on the track during qualifying and practice runs. But aside from what that data tell me, I mostly like to feel the car—to know it from the inside out. But in today's technologically advanced world of racing, though I can feel when something isn't right with the performance of the car, my engineer already knows exactly what the problems are and how to fix them before I'm off the track. Regardless, when the car is performing well, I'm happy with the feeling. When the car isn't right, no one is happy.

Once a race actually gets under way, I have to think about everything happening around me, outside the car, like when to come in for a pit stop and what kind of stop I'm making, whether it's a short stop or a long stop, changing tires or just adding fuel, or adjustments I want made to the car in my next pit. I am thinking about where the other drivers are on the track and the order we're all driving in, who's a lap down, whom I am racing against, and whom I will risk driving next to, especially if they are behind me in the standings. There's a lot happening inside the car too. I am constantly adjusting my suspension, monitoring all my engine functions, and adjusting my fuel mixture, switching between full power and various conservation levels according to the fuel strategies. Think of it this way; I'm literally driving the equivalent of an upside-down fighter jet. Of course, I like to say jet pilots are driving an upside-down IndyCar!

When you drive an open-cockpit car, there's a constant deluge of flying debris, including rubber from the tires, often referred to as marbles, exhaust fumes, oil on the track, stones or pebbles, and so on. Everything on the track becomes a potential hazard and a problem when it comes to seeing while I drive. Several times during the race I remove "tear offs," which are layered, plastic-like protectors that sit on top of the polycarbonate shield on my helmet to protect my eyes. With all this going on (and so much more . . .) I have to keep my mind clear so I can focus on what I have to do that day to compete, let alone win. One mistake can cost me the race—or worse. Racing is a rhythm—a cacophony of thought, skill, and teamwork. I know that a single lousy run, which would be merely a bad day for a male driver, could signify the end of my career, at least in the eyes of a lot of critics who were watching me in this race. People can write you off so easily in a sport like racing. If I have a good race, I'm considered "the next best thing." On the other hand, when things go less than stellar, I'm just another no-talent girl trying to fit in this "man's" sport. There was a lot riding on this race.

I knew I had what it would take to give the boys a good challenge. Like every other race of my career, I had something to prove. I know you can go from zero to hero and back again really fast. It's about staying consistent. That I did . . . all month long.

I'm one of those drivers who feeds off negativity a little bit, so I took all of the skeptics, all of the naysayers in the media, and all of the people who didn't believe I could win, and used them as my inspiration to go out there and show them what I'm made of—to prove to them that they were wrong: I could win. I knew that my presence in this race would make history—and in the end, it did.

With twenty-seven laps left to go in the four-hour-plus race, I found myself in the position I had hoped for, dreamed of, and wanted so much—I was in the lead for the second time that day. I led laps 172–175, dropping back to second place after Dan Wheldon passed me. Under yellow-flag conditions, my engineer Ray came on the radio and told me we'd need the restart of the century.

I told him, "Everybody say a prayer."

He radioed back, "We've been saying them all day!"

Somebody must have been listening, because I took over the lead from lap 188 to lap 194. I felt strangely comfortable. This is what I was built to do. The thought of winning was the culmination of a long and successful month. Admittedly, I made a lot of mistakes during that race—many due to my utter lack of experience as an Indy driver. As a rookie, I still had and have a lot to learn.

My first real setback came after lap 78, when I stalled my car coming out of the pits. I dropped to sixteenth place after racing my way up to fourth place. By lap 155, I had worked my way back up to seventh place. I was anxiously anticipating the green flag, as we were under a yellow warning again. At Indy, when we drive under a yellow flag, it is customary to accelerate between turns three and four. Whoever was leading the race seemed to have slowed down before he accelerated. As I came out of turn three, I didn't brake, even though there was a slowdown—I quickly turned and momentarily lost control of my car, which sent me spinning into the middle of the track and made me a moving target for the cars behind me, especially the car being driven by Thomas Enge, which broke the left front wing off of my car. My mishap caused the race to be put under caution, and the debris from my car left a trail of destruction behind me. Tomas Scheckter hit the wall trying to avoid the carnage, causing him to retire from the race after his crash. Thomas Enge and Tomas Scheckter, who did not finish as a result of my spin, were both victims of a chain reaction that started at the front of the pack. I was able to recover, but they were not.

I remained calm, returned to the pits, and sixty seconds later my car was fully repaired, with a new nose cone in place and wings attached, and I was back in the race. Four laps later, with the track still under a yellow caution flag, I returned to the pits to refuel and change all four of my tires. I found myself in ninth position after I returned to the race, and with forty-one laps to go. With the limited fuel I had, I knew I needed another caution flag if I had a prayer of winning. That would allow me to conserve fuel and finish without having to make another pit stop. My boss, Bobby Rahal, decided to roll the dice. It was now a race against fuel consumption. All eight cars ahead of me steered into the pits for their final refuel at lap 172. For the first time since lap 56, I was once again in the lead! I held off the pack by maintaining lap speed of 225 mph, lap after lap. There were two questions everyone wanted to know the answer to: Could any of the cars in the field catch me? And would I run out of fuel? Sixteen laps to go . . . 15 . . . 14 . . .

The morning of the race, Bob sat me down and told me that I had already exceeded his expectations. He told me to drive a smart race and do the best I could.

He said, "Let's go for Rookie of the Year."

It takes a rookie an average of thirty-three races to get his or her first win. I remember thinking that he had a point, and yet I had spent so many years waiting for this moment. My brain is wired to win—not place second, fourth, or tenth. My father's voice was ringing in my ears—"You're only as good as your last race."

I was more determined than ever to see this through—to be the first woman to win the coveted Indy 500.

At lap 186, Dan Wheldon nosed slightly ahead of me on the front stretch—just as yet another yellow flag unfurled after Kosuke Matsuura brushed the outside retaining wall between turns three and four. I would be able to conserve my fuel, as we raced three laps under caution. In my headset, my engineer informed me that I needed to conserve fuel. He told me that I could finish the race, but it was unlikely without a yellow flag and a lot of luck. I was faced with the dilemma of keeping the lead yet saving fuel, which meant not finishing the race at all. Like all decisions I make on the track, this had to be decisive and made in a split-second. As the fifteen cars still running positioned themselves at the bottom of the homestretch for a final restart, I knew what I had to do. I drafted Dan and blew past him on the restart. This would be the twenty-sixth lead change of the race. I wanted to give my team and the crowd the restart of the century . . . and I think I did just that.

I believed I had a real chance to win. Had another yellow flag come out, I probably would have. With six laps to go, Wheldon, whose car seemed to be running on more fuel than mine, hung with me until he finally passed me into turn one, never looking back. I decided to throttle down to conserve fuel, allowing two other cars to pass me. I finished in fourth place, a position I was pleased with for a rookie but disappointed with as a dreamer, a believer, and as someone who knows she has what it takes to win this race. I'm just a racer who happens to be a woman. I made several mistakes, but I am with a great team, and they helped me get back in the fight for the lead. At one point, I thought, "Wow, I could actually win this thing." I understood that both Dan Wheldon and Vitor Meira, who placed second, had more fuel to use, and it was very difficult to hold them off. But at the end of the day, I think I made my point. See you soon, boys!

After the front wing of my car was damaged hitting the side pod of Thomas Enge during lap 154 at the 2005 Indy 500, Panther Racing and I decided to auction it off on eBay and help raise some money for one of my favorite charities, Best Buddies Indiana, an organization that helps people with intellectual disabilities. I agreed to autograph the piece of racing memorabilia and hoped someone would want it. I wasn't sure anyone would want a racecar part, sold "as is," visibly damaged and unsuitable for framing. But apparently a few people cared—and cared a lot! The wing, which would cost around $5000 brand new, was sold to a very generous eBay bidder for $42,650.11! The fact that it came from my car contributed to the bidding frenzy. I signed the wing at the Bombardier LearJet 550 Texas Motor Speedway as "2005 Indianapolis 500 Rookie of the Year—Danica Patrick" and presented it to the winning bidder. I was thrilled to help raise money for a good cause and had a lot of fun along the way. I always had a feeling that both good things and bad things could happen if I performed well. In this case, something good (raising money for charity) came from an almost terrible situation. Luckily, I was able to continue the race and go on to finish fourth. I am now also in the Indianapolis Hall of Fame for my monumental broken wing, which was donated by the winning bidder.

Chapter ELEVEN

Taking the Time to Slow Down

I am beginning to learn that it is the sweet, simple things of life which are the real ones after all.

—*Laura Ingalls Wilder*

I'm not very good at quieting my mind. I can relax and chill out, but when it comes to quieting my thoughts and being in the moment, that takes work. I typically take thirty minutes and sometimes up to an hour in the morning to relax, sip my coffee, and welcome the new day. I find it to be useful time because I get peace and quiet before the regular hectic schedule of my day begins. Even on race days—in fact, especially on race days—I make sure I take an hour for breakfast. Emotions and energy levels can vary throughout the day, especially when you're busy doing all of the things you need to do. Making sure you take time to relax gives you an opportunity to ground yourself, to regain your focus and calm your mind. I use the mornings to do this because I feel that it sets the pace for the rest of my day. I start out feeling ready instead of crashing right into my obligations. I compartmentalize that time in the morning to provide a few minutes of relaxation because I know there is a time to rest and a time to work. I think having that time in the morning gives me more energy during the rest of the day to work.

Time is one of our most precious commodities. When I am not racing, my time is demanded by so many other people. But if you're a busy person on any level, learning to juggle your time and to balance yourself while you're being pulled in a lot of different directions is a challenge for all of us. Whether you're a working mom or dad, someone running a business, a student, or an employee of a company, we all have obligations at home and work. And many of us have additional obligations to those existing commitments, such as carpooling, attending a school play, playing an intramural basketball game, or doing volunteer work. If you're like me, you find that you are always giving your time to other people, and in the process of meeting those needs and obligations, you save very little if any of your time for yourself.

Inner peace is beyond victory or defeat.
                                                    —Bhagavad Gita

Lately I feel that I need "me time" all the time because my schedule is jammed, and especially during race season. The 2005 season was unusually challenging because a great portion of my time between race weekends was spent meeting obligations off the track. I found myself racing around on those days as if I had never gotten off the track—moving at speeds that feel natural when I am driving my car but are mind-swirling when I am being shuttled from the airport to a car, to meetings, to photo shoots, to interviews, back to the airports, just to start it all over again tomorrow.

> **Way too much coffee. But if it weren't for the coffee, I'd have no identifiable personality whatsoever.**
>
> **—David Letterman**

There is no way your mind and body can be fully charged when you have forgotten to plug in your battery. Think of it like your cell phone. Have you ever forgotten your battery charger? Panic sets in because your battery will never last through the next two days without it, right? You race around trying to find an open store to buy that charger because you can't be without your cell phone, right? Why would you take better care of your cell phone than you would of yourself?

Does the same kind of panic set in when you're dead tired and need to be recharged? If you're like most people, I am guessing the answer is "no." There is simply no way you can give, give, give, be all over the place, be busy every second of every day and be charged—fully charged. I can't do it. I don't know anyone who can.

There were so many days during the 2005 IRL season when I was dead tired and needed to sit—to just be still, to be in the opposite place to the one I'm in while driving. We all deserve a little self-indulgent "me time." Without it, you break down. And that's exactly what happened to me during the final week of my first Indy 500. After numerous public appearances, including television and media interviews, autograph sessions, and other obligations to promote the team and the league, I suddenly felt as if my body had shut down and said, "I can't do this anymore." It felt like a flu that unexpectedly set in, and at the worst possible time.

My body was telling me to stop, let up, give in. My mind was saying to keep going, full steam ahead. I was feeling very frustrated by the demands and pressure that had been placed on me before the race. I didn't feel like anything was mine anymore—not my time, not my opinions, and certainly not my needs. I had no opportunity to have my essential morning time, or any other time, to give myself a breather. Whether I wanted it to or not, my body simply shut down.

After returning to Indianapolis from a two-day trip to New York City, having done a nonstop round of talk shows, newspaper, print, magazine, and radio interviews, I was exhausted and mentally drained. I wasn't thinking clearly or rationally. I needed sleep. I needed a decent meal. I needed to get away from anyone who wanted something from me—no more interviews, no more cameras, no more obligations except racing. I called my publicist a jackass and accused him of trying to kill me on a golf cart, and I couldn't believe those words came out of my mouth. He was simply doing his job. This wasn't me. Was the pressure too much? Was I overwhelmed? Or was I exhausted from the endless obligations I had had no notion of before the month of May. I returned to the motor home that was my home during race weekends. It's where I can rest in between races and where my family and I spend time together on the road during the season. When I walked through the door after two long on-camera interviews with *CNN Live* and *NBC Nightly News*, I cracked. I bawled my eyes out for hours. After catching my breath, I asked my publicist to come to the motor home. I had to tell him I was sorry—I was, deeply. I cried again to him as I realized he was under a tremendous amount of pressure too. I don't think anyone expected the media monster that followed us throughout the month of May in Indianapolis.

I didn't recognize the person I had become that week. I didn't like the person staring back at me in the mirror, that's for sure. I had become resentful of the very thing that gave me the opportunities to have the life so many people dream of. The endless interviews and endless time given away was taking every ounce of energy that I had, and that I needed to excel on the track. Pressure in a racecar is something I'm very comfortable with. It was the pressure to keep giving and giving that got to me. I had no more to give—to anyone, not even myself. I always do whatever I need to do without a problem, so I never expected to break down. This was an emotional experience I'd never had. It was time to re-group, re-ground, and re-focus.

Everyone has his own kinds of breakdowns, for whatever reasons. It may seem inconceivable that interviews and television appearances are enough to break a tough chick like me, but in truth, haven't we all had a moment where we hit the proverbial wall, reach our breaking point?

Out of the blue, you simply say, "I can't take this anymore!"

Or, "I can't see you anymore"

Or, "I can't do this job anymore."

It was a seminal moment for me to recognize that I'm just human, and I have a wall, just like everyone else. I hit it—hard. Hitting a wall in a racecar is something I can usually walk away from. But there was no way I could just walk away from promises and obligations I had to my team, my sponsors, the Series, the race, and myself. I thought I could do it all. We've all been there. We all know what that feels like. It sucks. The big question, is what do you do after hitting that wall?

I allowed myself to break down for a few hours, behind closed doors, so no one else would know that I was having a weak moment. Remember, this was the week of the Indy 500. It was the culmination of all of my hard work for the past fourteen years. There were people doubting my racing ability, people who believed I didn't belong on the track, that I was out of my league, and people who simply wanted to see if I could win.

My breakdown gave me the downtime I needed to come back to the track the next day and place my focus on the task at hand. It also gave me perspective on how it feels when everything starts to spin out of my control. It gave me strong guidelines for how things needed to be handled in the future to ensure that I would no longer allow myself to become so over-committed that it negatively affected me personally, emotionally, and, most of all, professionally. Future races and personal commitments would have certain boundaries that would allow me to fulfill promises and not let anyone down, including myself. It is always better to under-promise and over-deliver.

Efficiency is concerned with doing things right. Effectiveness is doing the right things.
                                        —Peter F. Drucker

November 2005

Coming off my race season, I was excited to have the personal time to indulge myself in other areas of my life that needed my attention—specifically, my wedding day, which was a few weeks away. I was completely comfortable and justified in giving myself a break. I told everyone whose job it is to keep me busy that November would be a limited month—very limited in terms of what I would commit to professionally. My agent, my lawyer, my parents, and my team all supported my decision to focus on the most important day of my life.

Planning a wedding is a lot of work. Luckily Paul and I made most of the arrangements in January, before the start of the 2005 IRL season. I'm a good planner when it's something I am excited about. I was definitely giddy at the thought of marrying Paul, so making the arrangements never felt like work. It actually served as a positive distraction throughout the race season. By the time the season was over, unlike most brides-to-be I was able to relax and pamper myself a little before the big day.

I spent the weeks leading up to our nuptials celebrating with my mom, sister, and girlfriends, traveling to Napa for my bachelorette party, going over the fine details with Paul, and of course dieting to fit into my dress. I would have had a custom dress made, but I ordered the dress in January and didn't know if I would have the time for the fittings. On the other hand, since I had ordered the dress so early, I wanted to make sure it was going to fit, so aside from burning the soles of my sneakers off running and doing the elliptical, sweating my ass off doing yoga, and making the conscious decision to damage my skin with harmful UVA rays in a tanning booth, I also ate lots of fun and yummy foods (not!), including quinoa, cottage cheese, steamed vegetables with flax oil, and egg whites, and drank more water than Phoenix has seen . . . ever. The hardest part was my strict no-alcohol policy until the day I became Mrs. Hospenthal. (Coming soon: Danica's diet, detox, and deprivation book!)

November 19, 2005, 5:30 A.M.

I woke up feeling very calm, like it was any other morning. My sister, who was my maid of honor, came in from Illinois earlier that week to help me with the final details. My bridesmaids were coming to my house so that we could all have our hair and makeup done together. Brooke and I made a quick trip to the grocery store to get some very important items that were missing from my house. We picked up some fresh fruit, juices, and bagels, but our real mission was to get a couple bottles of champagne. We were successful. Back to the house we went. I made a pot of coffee, took a few sips, laced up my sneakers, and headed out for a brisk morning run—the sun hadn't yet come over the mountains out my back door.

My girls and my mom had already arrived by the time I returned from my run. Time to play beauty shop! We laughed, reminisced, read every gossip magazine Brooke and I could find at the store, while drinking mimosas. It was a very relaxing morning. Butterflies were elusive. I was filled with excited anticipation for becoming a Mrs.

We left for the church at 1:30, which was no easy task because my dress needed to stay clean and wrinkle-free. I held myself up in the limo by grasping the emergency handles above the doors as the driver seemed to make turn after turn, going an impossible 20 mph or less. Thank goodness for that upper-body strength I have from driving! It was all I could do not to yell from the back of the limo for the driver to step on it! I'm not used to traveling at those speeds.

Once I got to the church I began to get very anxious. I kept asking everyone the time?

"Is it time yet?"

"Is everyone ready?"

"I need lipstick. Where's Carlene?" (She was my makeup artist for the day.)

Guests were in place, and I was definitely ready. I think my parents were afraid of getting choked up moments before they walked me down the aisle, so I don't remember seeing a lot of them before the doors were swung open and "Here Comes the Bride" started playing.

Paul was standing at the altar, waiting with the groomsmen and bridal party. Our closest family and friends were on both sides of the aisle as I made my way toward him. It was all I could do to fight back the tears the moment he took my hand to walk me up to the altar. We said our vows and committed our lives to each other in the presence of our loved ones and God.

Inside the limo on the way to our reception, Paul and I toasted each other for the first time as Mr. and Mrs. Paul Hospenthal. We planned our reception to be as untraditional as we are. Our band, Cowboy Mouth, rocked the house. Paul and I cut loose and made our wedding night absolutely unforgettable. It was this little girl's dream come true.

I spend more than half of my year away from home, and these days, as a newlywed, home is a place I love to be. Home represents a peaceful place in my otherwise hectic life. I thoroughly enjoy making coffee, spending quiet time with Paul before he leaves for work, and creating a warm, peaceful home for us to build our lives in together.

I still find the road a very lonely place. When I am not racing, it's the last place I want be. Thankfully, my husband is able to travel with me, so we are rarely apart. Even when we're at a race, Paul, my parents, and I will usually hang around the motor home we travel in, grilling and sharing family time because it gives us a sense of "home" on the road.

Being on my own has given me an unusual level of maturity for someone my age. I was put on the fast track of learning the lessons of life. Living on the road, you learn that a bend in the road is not necessarily the end of the road. You learn to cope with the twists and turns—when to grab the wheel tighter, when to hug the line, and when to go wider. These days I don't have to worry about navigating the course alone because my husband is with me, by my side, making this journey with me. I will never be alone again—and what a feeling that is.

Chapter TWELVE

Rock What You've Got

You see things; and you say, "Why?" But I dream
things that never were; and I say, "Why not?"

—*George Bernard Shaw*

Looking Back

Indy Racing League Trackside Administration Office,
Indianapolis, Indiana, May 2005
A large stack of fan mail is delivered to the office. On the top of the
pile is a letter simply addressed:

Danica Patrick
Indianapolis Motor Speedway
Indianapolis, Indiana

Who? Hey, that's me! Wow. All I can say is what a ride!

The year 2005 was one to remember. I never knew that life could be this good. I am incredibly lucky and blessed. I am whole in so many areas of my life at one time. While I tried to keep my focus and my eyes on the prize, there were a lot of unexpected honors and special opportunities that accompanied my rookie season. When *Automotive News* named their 100 Leading Women in the North American Auto Industry, the 2005 honorees included seven CEOs, three COOs, thirteen presidents, fifty-two vice presidents, four assembly plant managers, and one racecar driver—me. I almost felt out of place!

When Marquis Who's Who released its 2006 edition of *Who's Who in America*, who could have guessed I would have something in common with Nobel Peace Prize–winning physicists, Kanye West, iPod designer Jonathan Ive, and actress Eva Longoria? (Not that I mind the comparisons!)

I was named Female Athlete of the Year, voted on by the United States Sports Academy and USA Today.com. I beat out Maria Sharapova, the Williams sisters, and Michelle Wie, just to name a few. I was stunned! I went to my first Hollywood premier, for *Herbie: Fully Loaded*. I was also invited as both nominee and presenter to the 2005 ESPY Awards, given for excellence in sports performance. I was up for Best Breakthrough athletic performance for the year. Once again, I was up against Maria Sharapova, who won Wimbledon in 2004, Ben Roethlisberger of the Pittsburgh Steelers, and Dwyane Wade of the Miami Heat. Though I didn't win (Dwyane Wade did), just to be nominated with a group of successful athletes was a great honor. I was seated in the second row, and as I looked around to see all of the athletes and celebrities who were there, I suddenly realized Paul and I had better seats than Nick and Jessica!

I appeared twice on *The Late Show* with my boss, David Letterman, ESPN's *SportsCenter, Pardon the Interruption, The Today Show, CNN, The Tony Danza Show, Jimmy Kimmel Live, Good Morning America, CBS Evening News, World News Tonight,* and just about every other talk show on the air . . . except Jay Leno. He asked, but I had to graciously decline.

When it takes so long to achieve a goal, you begin to understand that the journey is the goal. In life, there is no guaranteed destination. I always knew I'd someday drive in the Indy 500. I knew from my earliest childhood memories that I would make a name for myself as a professional racecar driver. If everything went right, I believed I could have a positive impact on whatever series I drove for. I put all of my effort and attention toward striving for my goals—small and large. When all of your hard work and perseverance finally does pay off, you can never—ever—take it for granted. Fame, fortune, popularity, and success all come and go. I know people will forget me as fast as they learned about me, but they will never be able to deny my contributions to the sport, to racing history, to opening doors for women and all athletes coming up right behind me. I've been told that there has been a dramatic increase in young girls wanting to take up karting, and that thrills me, knowing I might have had an influence in their decision to race around a track against the boys.

It's not work if you love what you're doing.
—*Steve Sears*

Danica Patrick

I didn't expect to fall into the position of "role model" so quickly. I have never gone out there to try and be someone other than who I am. This is my job. It's not about proving that men are inferior or women are exactly the same as men. The inspirational aspect of my role took me quite by surprise. I surely never set out to be an inspiration to anyone but myself. It wasn't until I started receiving fan mail and email, and meeting young kids at races that I realized there is a tremendous responsibility that comes with being "different" and with being "famous." The truth is, I'm not doing anything different than I've always done, and I won't do anything different because that is exactly what got me to where I am today. That's the inspiration. It's just me. No excuses. No apologies. The best part of being a role model and walking through life being exactly who I am, is that I don't have to worry about anyone "finding out" something about me that isn't already out there or that I don't portray by walking my talk.

From time to time, I try to take a look at my life, and see the whole picture: what I've already done, where I've been, records I've already broken and set. It helps keep me humble and gives me perspective on how far I've come. It's my hope for the future that brings me back to dreaming and aspiring to all the unknown that has yet to come. The past is sealed. It's done. The future is boundless and full of opportunity. The promise of my future keeps me trying as hard as I can, and knowing that when you reach for the stars, you might get over the fence.

People ask me all the time why I race? I race cars because it's what I am good at. We all like to do things we are good at. I also like the originality of me in racing.

I like to be different.

I like the challenge of the sport and relish that I'm underestimated.

I can hardly wrap my brain around the swirl of attention that followed me during my IRL rookie season. The media frenzy was unbelievable. In January 2006, I was given the opportunity to drive in the endurance race called the 24 hours of Daytona. This race is an incredibly historic and sought-after victory for any driver from any series. My Daytona team consisted of Rusty Wallace, a freshly retired champion NASCAR driver; Tony Stewart, the 2005 NASCAR champion; past Formula One driver Alan McNish; and past 24 hours of Daytona winner Rob Dyson, just to name a few. This particular year, the race was especially historic because every team had the most respected drivers and talent from all over the world, and the roster featured every form of car raced today.

To be part of this was a huge honor and a great experience. I drove a Daytona Prototype car, which is completely different from open-wheel. It's a closed-cockpit car, with a top speed of 190 mph. For a driver to be able to jump into a different car than she's used to and perform well shows what kind of driver she is. I was happy to walk away with an open invitation to come back and do it again for one of the best teams in the series. A few days after the race, I took a look at the experience and was very proud of what I had done and was amazed that among all of these world-famous drivers, the fans came out to cheer me on, and the racers made me feel very welcome in their world. It felt like the level of media attention and fan interest from last year never went away. I was just back at the track, being who I was born to be—a driver.

Was it because I was one of the most high-profile women racers in

Daytona? Or was it because I am one of a few female athletes today setting the standard that women can compete in male-dominated sports? Whatever the reason, it felt very rewarding. Lots of women have come along over the years to show the world that, yes, we are women, hear us roar—athletes from Billie Jean King to Julie Krone to more contemporary athletes like Mia Hamm and Michelle Wie. They each have proved that women can and will continue to be fierce competitors.

> **I'm tough, I'm ambitious, and I know exactly what I want. If that makes me a bitch, OK.**
> *—Madonna*

Throughout sports history, women have had to work with male-dominated sports organizations and structures in order to participate. The first modern Olympics, held in 1896, did not allow women to participate. I am glad I was born in 1982! When women were allowed to participate, in 1900, it was in only three sports: golf, archery, and tennis. Out of the 1225 athletes, only nineteen were women. It is hard to believe that there was a time when women were not allowed in the pit or garage areas of the Indianapolis 500. Janet Guthrie made racing history in 1977 as the first woman to compete in the prestigious race. I imagine my experience in 2005 was much different. Every time I stopped my car in the pit lane, fans were cheering, and when I got out of my car, everywhere I walked they were asking for my autograph, which I was happy to give as much as I could. They were clearly embracing my presence. I'm not sure what Janet dealt with, but I know there was resistance to women racing, something I rarely deal with. We've definitely come a long way, baby!

Until recent years, women have been regarded as the "weaker" sex. A woman's role in society was to be submissive, passive, and obedient to men. A good athlete has talent regardless of gender. Despite my role and position as the only woman racing in the IRL, I have never emphasized that I am a female driver, nor am I in the sport to illustrate or grow and promote the "power of women." I promote skill, talent, drive, ambition, and determination in whatever form. While it still confuses me that female athletes receive less money for endorsements, scholarships, and earnings, nothing will change until women prove that they can be equal competition and draw the same crowds as men's sporting events. It is the fans' demand for an athlete that dictates our earnings. Either way, women are not going away—we're getting stronger.

What is the point of having slightly different rules for women and men? Many women athletes contend that the rules of the game change slightly for women as soon as it appears that women are catching up. It certainly has been an issue when it comes to my size and weight driving an IndyCar. Drivers complain that I have an "unfair" advantage because I am smaller and lighter than the average male driver, giving me a slight advantage in speed because my car could potentially go 1/10 of a mile an hour faster for every ten pounds of difference. While that may be true, what I lack in weight I have to more than make up for in body strength. Should I complain that men are stronger than I am and therefore they have an unfair advantage driving? I don't think so.

Gentleman, start your excuses!

Quit your whining boys. Drive. Prove you're better or I will.

Giving Back

As success came, so did my responsibility to balance the scale. I did this by making sure I gave something back. It has always been important for me to give back—especially when it comes to those intangible things such as kindness, humility, compassion, wisdom, experience, and education. I do my best to give everything I have to offer on the track to my race team, to the series, to sponsors, and most important, to myself.

Writing this book is an opportunity for me to motivate, inspire, and even change someone's life. If this book touches only a few people in a positive way, that will be a reward beyond any material benefit. I believe God gave me abilities as a racecar driver with a platform to speak to people of all ages, men and women alike. I have a rare opportunity to cross the line and bridge a gap that separates men and women. I've only just begun to share my spirit and my hope that someday we will live in a world where a woman can grow to become president of the United States and little boys can grow up believing it's not a mark of inferiority to stay home and raise children while their wives run the country!

Looking Forward

People ask me if I weren't a racecar driver, what would I do? Thankfully, I've never had to think about that! I am just beginning to make my mark. I continue to learn from each and every race, at the only rate I know—mine. I don't feel that I need to go any faster or win any sooner, though it would be nice. With all the hype and hope for a win, I think people know it takes a long time to win a race, any race—on or off the track. Life is a race—your job is a race. Everything we do ultimately comes down to trying our hardest to get the results we hope to achieve. You don't have to drive a racecar to know you're in the race. All that matters is that you're in the game.

There is nothing I want to do more than win. That has been one consistent motivating force in my life. My desire to be successful and to win has been the same forever. There are more things written about me than about some of the other drivers, but that doesn't make me want to do better. I think all athletes at the top level try as hard as they can all the time or they are not the best—they are at the back of the pack, looking for success but lacking the commitment to be number one. Do you remember when you were growing up playing a sport with someone who didn't take losing lightly? Maybe he or she was a little too competitive, too aggressive. That person may grow up to be the next Shaquille O'Neal, Peyton Manning, or Tiger Woods. I know I was that person. Don't be afraid of competition. Those players only make you a stronger and better athlete. Embrace their spirit and try to take some of their drive for your own benefit.

What is it about racing that I can never let go of? Is it the competition? Is it about the control? I do like control. Yeah, in all areas of my life. But according to Nicole Kidman's character in the movie *Days of Thunder*, control is an illusion. I have to agree. Ask any racecar driver how quickly he or she can lose control on or off the track, and you will be told in less than a hundredth of a second. So more than control, I race because there is a drive inside me that makes me think I am better than the other guy and can do anything I set my mind to. Racing is a sport in which the highs are high, but few and far between, and the lows are really low and occur more often. But I don't care. Racing is my drug of choice. It's a part of my being. It starts at my innermost core and works its way out through everything I do. I love racing. If you love something or someone enough, that really is all you need. That love will carry you through the toughest and most trying times, and will embrace you in moments of joy and victory. My greatest accomplishments so far have been achieving my goal to become a professional racecar driver and marrying Paul. What do those two parts of my life have in common? L-o-v-e. Love is *all* you need.

Rock What You've Got

Getting my break as a driver had nothing to do with being an attractive female, but to be honest, it didn't hurt me either. Sponsors recognized that it was a potential plus for them and that I fit their campaign or the direction they were going. It worked. It was a win-win for everyone. Even if someone is the most popular athlete in the world, if a company is not marketing to athletes or that athlete's demographic, he or she won't be a fit, regardless of his or her status or draw. No company will sign me as a spokeswoman if I don't offer a benefit to its marketing strategy. Talent and marketability are individually based. Female or male, as athletes, we still have to do our job, and we have to fit a particular marketing plan for sponsors to get behind us. For me, just being a woman isn't going to do it. I still have to perform. Some women in sports have remained reluctant to use their looks or their femininity to capitalize or exploit their roles. I say, don't be afraid. Use what God gave you—*You gotta rock what you've got.*

When I came back from England, I experienced the longest time I ever went without a ride. What finally got me my contract with Team Rahal? My confidence, my strong handshake, and my relentless determination to succeed. I never gave up. That experience of being without a ride, of facing the notion of possibly never racing again, was the catalyst to becoming who I am, and it determined how I got to where I am today. Because I had the unconditional support of my family and retained my resolve to be successful and the good sense to never take "no" for an answer, I was able to achieve my dream of driving professionally.

The mentors of today were the women racers of yesterday, and the women racers of today, including myself, are tomorrow's mentors. It's a role I am prepared for if it means more young women grow up believing they can do anything, be anyone, and achieve everything they aim for—it they can grow up believing that nothing is impossible.

It is certainly my responsibility, and one of the best parts of breaking down barriers and crossing these imaginary lines for future generations. That's just what the barriers are—imaginary. Don't let history or society dictate what you can and cannot do or what is normal and okay. I never will.

Danica Patrick
Career Highlights

2005

- Named 2005 Indianapolis 500 Rookie of the Year.

- Became the highest-qualifying (fourth) and -finishing (fourth) female driver in the history of the Indianapolis 500, led nineteen laps of the race, becoming the first woman to ever lead the Indy 500.

- Was the first IndyCar driver to be featured on the cover of *Sports Illustrated* in twenty years.

- Named the Bombardier IRL IndyCar Series Rookie of the Year.

- Tied the IRL IndyCar Series mark for poles won by a rookie (three). Was the second female driver to win an IndyCar Series pole position, and the only woman in history to win three in one season, capturing the pole position at the Argent Indy 300 at

Kansas Speedway, the Amber Alert Portal Indy 300 at Kentucky Speedway, and Chicagoland Raceway.

- Started at an impressive second place at Motegi, Japan, and led for thirty-two laps before finishing fourth.

- Started on the front row at Nashville and led for nine laps before finishing in seventh place, her fifth top-ten result in the first nine races.

- Nominated for Best Breakthrough athlete for the 2005 ESPY Awards.

- Named the second most influential driver in motorsports by *Racer* magazine.

- Named as one of the 100 Leading Women in the North American Automotive Industry by *Automotive News* magazine.

- Named a finalist for Sportsman of the Year by the Women's Sports Foundation.

2004

- Finished third in the Toyota Atlantic Championship, posting 269 points and ten top-five results in twelve races in the Argent Mortgage Toyota/Swift. Was the only driver in the Toyota Atlantic Series to complete every lap of the season.

- Became the first female driver to win a pole position in the Toyota Atlantic when she collected her first Atlantic pole position for round 5 at Portland.

- Collected three podium results in 2004, finishing on the podium (third) at Monterrey, Mexico, second at Portland (round 4), and third at Cleveland.

- At Denver (round 10), captured the Argent Fast Lap Award for posting the fastest race lap en route to a fourth-place finish.

2003

- Piloted the Argent Mortgage Company Toyota/Swift to a sixth-place finish in the Toyota Atlantic Championship.

- Claimed a pair of podium results and five top-five results in her rookie campaign.

- Became the first female to post a podium (top-three) result in the thirty-year history of the Atlantic series with a third-place finish at Monterrey, Mexico.

- Posted three impressive top-five results at Cleveland, Trois Rivières, and Denver.

- Posted a season-best, second-place finish at Miami, where she ran a single American Le Mans Series (ALMS) race for the British Prodrive team in late June at Road Atlanta.

2002

- Signed a multi-year driving contract with Team Rahal. Was tabbed as the team's driver for a Toyota Atlantic entry in 2003.

- As preparation for her full-season effort in 2003, ran a limited Barber–Dodge Pro Series schedule of five races. Made her debut at Toronto, qualifying eleventh and finishing seventh. Collected her highest finish of the Barber-Dodge Pro Series with a fourth-place finish at Vancouver.

- Successfully tested a Busch Grand National car with PPC Racing.

- Captured the pole for the 2002 Long Beach Grand Prix Toyota Pro/Celebrity Race and won the pro division, topping former Trans Am champion Tommy Kendall and IRL driver Sarah Fisher.

2001

- Won the Gorsline Scholarship Award for the top upcoming road-racing driver.

- Was recognized as the top female open-wheel driver in racing with extraordinary international experience.

- Competed in England, driving in the British Zetek Formula Ford Championship. Returned to the U.S. searching for a top open-wheel ride and had successful test runs in USAC Midget, Toyota Atlantic, and ALMS cars.

2000

- Finished an astonishing second at the Formula Ford Festival in England, the highest finish ever for an American in the event, surpassing the previous record-setting performance of Danny Sullivan. Drove for Andy Welch in the British Zetek Formula Ford.

- Competed in Championship Racing in England for Haywood Racing in the European Formula Ford Series.

- Served as the lead test driver for the Haywood Racing and Mygale Factory Team.

1999

- Finished ninth in the Formula Vauxhall Championship in England, her first full season in the UK.

1998

- Made her racing debut in England at age sixteen driving in the Formula Vauxhall Winter Series.

- Ran a limited karting schedule while she attended the Formula Ford racing school in Canada.

1997

- In her final full season of karting, captured the World Karting Association (WKA) Grand National championship, HPV class.

- Won the WKA Grand National championship in the Yamaha Lite class.

- Won the WKA Summer National championship in the Yamaha Lite class.

- Finished tenth in the Elk Constructors championship in Formula A.

1996

- Established herself as a rising star in karting by winning thirty-nine of her forty-nine featured races.

- At the age of fourteen, won the WKA Manufacturers Cup National Points title in the Yamaha Junior and Restricted Junior class. Was the runner-up for the WKA Manufacturers Cup National Points title (HPV 100 Junior) and the WKA Grand National Championship (Yamaha Restricted Junior).

- Captured five WKA Great Lakes Sprint Series and WKA Midwest Spring Series titles.

- Won the IKF Division 7 event in Willow Springs, California (Yamaha Junior), and finished second in the IKF Grand Nationals in the Yamaha Junior group.

1995

- Won the WKA Great Lakes Sprint Series title (Yamaha Restricted Junior and U.S. 820 Jr.) while placing second in WKA Manufacturers Cup National Points in the same categories.

1994

- At the age of twelve captured her first national points championship in the WKA Manufacturers Cup in the Yamaha Sportsman class. Collected the WKA Grand National Championship in the Yamaha class and won the WKA Great Lakes Sprint Series in the Yamaha Sportsman and US820 Sportsman classes.

1993

- In her second season of karting, finished second in the WKA Midwest Sprint Series in both the Yamaha and US820 classes. Finished fourth in the WKA Manufacturers Cup national points in the Yamaha Sportsman class.

1992

- Began her karting career at the age of ten. Was lapped six laps into her first event but finished the season second in the points championship out of twenty drivers.

Danica Patrick Individual Professional Race Results

IRL IndyCar Series

2005 Season Results

Indy 500 Rookie of the Year after becoming the first woman to lead the Indy 500 and ending the race as the highest qualifying and finishing woman.

Year: Rookie

Starts: 13

Poles: 2

Wins: 0

Top-five results: 2

Top-ten results: 6

Laps led: 60

Danica Patrick

2004 Season Results
    Starts: 12
    Pole position: 1
    Podiums: 3
    Top five: 10
    Top ten: 12
    Season result: Third in the championship

2003 Season Results
    Starts: 12
    Podiums: 2
    Top five: 5
    Top ten: 10
    Season result: Sixth in the championship

Danica's Diary

March 3, 2005, First Day in the IRL Practice,
Toyota Indy 300 Homestead–Miami Speedway, Homestead, Florida

It's my first Indy Car race and I'm pretty nervous. I didn't have the best day out there. I wasn't as fast as I was when I tested at this track earlier in the year. Hopefully, we'll figure out how to make the car go faster and be ready for qualifying tomorrow. I need to remember why I'm here and that is because I can drive a racecar. I know I've got a lot to learn, but if I can just make it through this first day without a mistake, I'll be able to build on it and move forward.

March 6, 2005, Toyota Indy 300,
Homestead–Miami Speedway, Homestead, Florida

What a shitty day. I qualified ninth, which I was pretty happy with. Then I dropped back early in the race but was able to work my way forward right back to where I started. With forty laps to go, the green flag comes back out after a caution. The last thing I remember is going below the white line to go around the accident happening in turn one and then boom! I got hit. I can't remember anything else. I was so pissed. What I thought was going to be a great first race ended worse than I could have imagined. I just hope I get cleared to race in Phoenix.

March 19, 2005, XM Satellite Radio Indy 200, presented by Argent Mortgage, Phoenix International Raceway, Phoenix, Arizona

I got cleared to race, but I'm not sure I'm happy about it. This was the hardest race I've ever done. Every time I got even close to the back end of someone, it felt like the nose of the car was pinned to the ground and the rear was going to come around. This makes for a long day on a short oval when all you do is turn. But, in the end, I finished, and that really was the goal. We all knew the cars weren't that great, so everyone was happy that I just brought it home. Task # 1 . . . to finish a race . . . ✓

April 3, 2005, Honda Grand Prix of St. Petersburg, St. Petersburg, Florida

So I finally ran in the front at some point during the race this weekend. I held my own in second place until I needed fuel. I came back out on the track and accidentally turned the pit speed limiter back on. I couldn't go any faster than 60 mph. I felt so stupid once I turned it off, and even more stupid that I wrecked the gearbox trying to find a gear that would speed up my car. I was surprised how quickly my crew changed the gearbox. Five laps later, I was back on the track. My accomplishment today was running up front for a little while and walking away with the Rookie of the Year lead.

April 30, 2005, Indy Japan 300, Motegi, Japan

I love Japan! The people are nice, the food is good, and Paul and I have had a lot of time together. I'm a little nervous because this track isn't like Homestead or Phoenix. Each end of the track is different; one end is really fast and wide and the other end is much tighter. I asked Buddy to take me around the track in a road car and show me the lines, which helped me a lot. The team has done really well here, so I'm optimistic.

May 3, 2005, Indianapolis Motor Speedway, Indianapolis, Indiana

Indy is here! I have been waiting for this day for a long time. It is exciting, but I'm walking into this month as if it's just another race that I'm trying to win. I have to say, I have a pretty good feeling coming from a fourth place in Japan and being with the defending Indy 500 team. That's a good place to start. First stop . . . rookie orientation, where I tell all of us who have never driven here before that we have to slowly build speed 5 mph at a time, starting at 190 mph. I'm told it's pretty easy. Let's hope so.

Danica Patrick

May 10, 2005

What a shocker of a day. Buddy hit the wall, rear end first, in turn two. Lots of people have been crashing there, but his was the biggest. I saw his steering wheel after the car came back to the garage, and it was bent and broken. He must have been holding on tight. All it takes in racing is hitting slightly wrong, and you end up in the hospital. I know how that feels. I went to see Buddy at the hospital, and he seemed OK and chatty. But no one knows if he's going to get back in the car this month.

May 28, 2005

Not much time to write. I think my life just changed today. I'm not sure what's going on, but everyone seems pretty happy—even I'm smiling a little. I do know for a fact I made some history today by leading the 500. Now it's time to let loose! I just finished my <u>Sports Illustrated</u> shoot, and I'm going to dinner with Paul, my family, and my agent, Lynn.

June 11, 2005, Bombardier Lear Jet 550K,
Texas Motor Speedway, Fort Worth, Texas

I'm starting to realize the impact that Indy had. All the drivers had a mandatory autograph session today, and there were so many people there, officials handed out wristbands. The track was no exception for fans either. There were over 100,000 people on this very hot Saturday night. I qualified third, which was good since we are still struggling with the car a little bit. The race was a different story. I dropped back quickly and couldn't get my car to handle right and be comfortable to drive. At least I did a little more side-by-side racing and got more comfortable with that. I finished thirteenth and I'm still leading the Rookie of the Year points.

June 25, 2005, SunTrust Indy Challenge,
Richmond International Raceway, Richmond, Virginia

My biggest concern going into the weekend was the physical demand of this track. I'm as prepared as I can be. I just hope it's enough. All the short ovals I've done in my career have been fairly difficult. I'm crossing my fingers this is not what holds me back this weekend. I was the slowest car. There is nothing worse than being slowest. The only thing that made me excited about qualifying was that someone didn't get a time (he crashed), so I was second to last—and not totally last. The race was actually OK for me. I didn't get tired, and I came home with a top-ten finish. Ray and I had hoped for a top ten, and said that we would be happy if that happened. It did.

Danica Patrick

I am pretty happy to be back at a big track since I've been pretty unsuccessful at road courses and short ovals. I know as a rookie, I'm going to have some good races and some bad ones, but it doesn't make me feel better at the moment. It did turn around for me in qualifying, though. I got my first pole. YEAH! I know my work has only begun, but I'm starting at the best spot possible. It makes me feel even better to know that to my right is Buddy and directly behind me is Vitor. As a team we kicked ass. During the race, I can't say it was easy, but I did learn. The car had quite a bit of understeer and is not that great on cold tires, so I dropped back to ninth on the start. The pit stops hurt me pretty bad today, but I hung in there all day and did a lot of battling with Helio. The gears felt a little off, so passing was a challenge, but not impossible. I ended up in ninth place. Once again, I'm disappointed, but I learned a little bit about how to make a car handle and even more about side-by-side racing.

July 13, 2005: My 'ESPY Diary

I guess you could say Memorial Day weekend changed my life. After finishing fourth at Indy I've been invited to a lot of cool functions and events. The honor of being invited to the ESPY Awards was twice as nice because I was invited as both a nominee and as a presenter. I presented with Patrick Dempsey of _Grey's Anatomy_, who just happens to be a big fan of the IndyCar Series.

My day started early with a 6:00 A.M. flight from Phoenix to LA. At noon, I met with the ESPN Style Studio at the Mondrian Hotel. The Style Studio is every girl's dream come true. Hair, makeup, nails—you know, the works—for FREE! The people who ran the Style Studio were awesome and took great care of me. At 4 o'clock, I had about thirty minutes to get dressed before Paul and I had to leave the Mondrian and walk the red carpet at the Kodak Theatre. When I arrived the red carpet was in full swing, with lots of celebrities and athletes doing interviews and signing autographs for the fans. This was so much cooler than it looks on TV, but a lot of hard work! It took so long to get down the red carpet that the ESPY people came to get me because I had to be in my seat for the start of the show. Thank goodness I was wearing a pair of comfy Manolos. Being late meant I missed my rehearsal with the teleprompter, so the producers came to get me so I could pre-read my script. The show was being taped for television, and I didn't want to mess up.

I was up for Best Breakthrough athlete, which was early in the show. I had a good feeling, but Dwyane Wade won. Right after I went backstage and got ready to present the Best Male Olympic Performance. It was cool that it went to a fellow Argent Mortgage–sponsored athlete, Olympic swimmer Michael Phelps.

The show was long, but it was really cool. The night was literally a who's who of sports, with people like Tyrell Owens, LeBron James, Annika Sorenstam, Peyton Manning, and, oh yes, the actual winner of the Indy 500, Dan Wheldon. Ha-ha. Mix in Hollywood stars like Matthew Perry, Oprah Winfrey, Jessica Simpson, Nick Lachey, Jessica Beil, Patrick Dempsey, Wilmer Valderrama, and Destiny's Child, and it was a really fun evening I'll never forget. It would have been great to hang out and see more people, but the IndyCar Series doesn't give you a weekend off to live the Hollywood life. I was off the next morning at 5:45 A.M. to catch a flight to Nashville for the Firestone Indy 200. Now that's what I call life in the fast lane!

July 16, 2005, Firestone Indy 200,
Nashville SuperSpeedway, Nashville, Tennessee

I know I'm supposed to be happy starting on the front row, but I'm not. Our qualifying was rained out, so when they went off of practice times, I was second by only a couple hundredths. I really think if we had qualified, I would have had another pole. Oh well. Again, on the start, I had to deal with cold tires, and the Panoz is pretty bad on cold tires. That's why I always drop back on the starts. I dealt with a lot of understeer, and with each pit stop, we tried to make it better, but it wasn't quite enough. Because of our fuel strategy, I led for a little while, but couldn't make it last. When the yellow flag came out, it started to rain and I thought the race was going to be over. The rain stopped just in time for a few green-flag laps to finish the race. I kept my foot in it and finished seventh.

July 24, 2005, The Milwaukee Mile, West Allis, Wisconsin

I have to say, I drove really well this weekend. I was the fastest Panoz by a long way. I qualified sixth and barely dropped back at all during the race. I was leaning really hard into the traction control. A little after halfway I came into the first corner like I had been, but this time, for some reason, the rear of the car came around and I hit the wall. After looking at some replays, I really think I hit some oil—at least that's what I'm telling myself. All in all, from an attack standpoint, this was probably one of my best races yet.

Danica Patrick

July 31, 2005, Michigan Indy 400,
Michigan International Speedway, Brooklyn, Michigan

Gosh! Where do I start? I felt like if I was going to win, so far this race would be my best opportunity. The track is big and fast, just like Indy. Practice # 1: I wasn't sure if I had forgotten how to drive or if I was really smart but I could not keep my foot down the whole way around the track, and it's supposedly really easy. In fact, I couldn't keep it down the whole weekend. The tires we got were different than before and they gave our car tons of oversteer. I managed to qualify eighth, which wasn't too bad considering how I had been running. For the first fifty laps of the race, I was just trying to save my life. I felt like I was back at Phoenix, with a car that was trying to spin me out. I managed to work with my tools inside the car and made it a tolerable racecar. I was about to pass someone down the inside into turn three, and my engine blew. Instead of continuing round and round, I pulled straight into the pits. My day was over.

August 14, 2005, Bluegrass 300, Kentucky Speedway, Sparta, Kentucky

Another pole! Woo hoo! Even though it came from a rainout situation. I guess karma comes around because I lost the pole in Nashville due to rain. I was fast. I had the car figured out and was in the strongest position since Indy to win a race. A yellow flag came out, and as I downshifted to enter the pits, the sound was not good. After I came back on the track from my pit stop, I couldn't get any of my top gears. I'm not going to go too far with only a couple gears. Once again, the crew had to change the gearbox. When I got back on the track I was told to not pass anyone, and I said on the radio, "What's the point of being out here?" The Series ended up allowing me to pass, and I worked my way all the way back up to the lead pack. Again, I was fast, but I need to learn to be careful with my equipment, or I am never going to finish.

August 21, 2005, Honda Indy 225,
Pikes Peak International Raceway, Fountain, Colorado

Here we go again. Another short oval. What should I expect from this one? In the first practice, I couldn't believe it, but I was able to hold my foot all the way down to the floor the whole way around. That was pretty fast. Wah-hoo! I started fifth and held my own all day on the track even though the tires went off pretty badly at the end of each fuel run. The biggest setback all day was a restart where I had to start in the back for some odd reason. I wasted so much time getting by lap traffic that the lead group got away and I only finished eighth. I guess I should smile thinking about the other two short ovals—so I'm going to.

Danica Patrick

August 28, 2005, Argent Mortgage IndyCar Grand Prix, Infineon Raceway, Sonoma, California

If I thought Richmond was physically tough, boy, was I stupid. I fully admit on this piece of paper, Sonoma was BRUTAL. Not only was it physically tough, but we couldn't seem to get the car to handle right. I couldn't brake well. I couldn't carry speed through a corner. And I couldn't get out of it. That pretty much takes care of the whole track. My goal was to just finish. We tried to be clever with strategy and stayed out during the first full-course yellow. I was in second place and knew I was going to get passed, but I didn't think someone was going to drive into the side of me to do it. What was he thinking? Stupid idiot! And that's exactly what I said on the radio after I got hit. What else is there to say. Bad, bad, bad day.

September 11, 2005, Chicagoland Speedway, Joliet, Illinois

Woo hoo! Pole #3. I am so proud of myself. This was definitely my best race of the year so far. I really feel like I'm getting a handle on how to make the car feel good with full fuel, with old tires, and with cars around me. I'm getting braver and it's paying off. I legitimately ran up front all day—not because of pit stops, or strategy, or because cars fell out of the race. There were only fifteen laps to go and we were under full-course

202

caution. When the green flag came out, I was a little bit over-anxious. I nearly took the lead before we even got out of turn four from fourth place. Hey, I was trying! Since my tires had done two full stints, I could barely keep the car on the bottom of the track. So I drove up high, but that leaves the door open for passing. I dropped back to sixth but managed to hold off Vitor to the checkered flag.

September 25, 2005, Watkins Glen Indy GP, presented by Argent, Watkins Glen International Raceway, Watkins Glen, New York

After my performances on the road courses so far, I'd be lying if I said I was looking forward to this race. After flying to New York the week before the race and starting a huge media tour, I came down with a horrible cold. I was taking so much Suphedrine during the day and Nyquil at night I'm not sure I was myself. The race didn't make me feel any better. After struggling to make the car fast, I started from sixth. I actually worked my way up to the top ten. Buddy had a problem and the yellow flag came out. As I drove by him on the back straight, I have no idea how I did it, but I switched the ignition off! My hand was telling me, "STOP! GO HOME!" I pulled off to the side, since my car wasn't running, and couldn't figure out what happened until I went to turn my ignition off and it already was! Wow. Did I feel stupid. Not to mention Buddy and myself having problems, and Vitor had an electrical problem on the same lap as well. All I could do at that point was drive as hard as I could and just finish the race. The only sunshine to that day was the fact that I locked up Rookie of the Year. It was very hard to be excited, but I managed to realize for a second I had achieved something that day.

October 16, 2005, Toyota Indy 400,
California Motor Speedway, Fontana, California

It's the last race of the year. C'mon, Danica! Finish strong. Practice went pretty good. We were fast. My eyes were on the record for most amount of poles in a rookie season three was the record. One to go. To my disappointment, the gears were way off for qualifying. The wind was so much different than we thought it was going to be. Fifth gear was way too short and sixth gear was way too long. Since the rev limiter doesn't get you very far, I left it in sixth gear and lugged the car as smoothly as I could around the track. Even with the problem, I still qualified fourth, but man, was I pissed. I worked my butt off and made my way forward, but every time I came into the pits, I lost more than I made up. The car felt pretty good, but it wasn't good enough to blow past everyone all day. A yellow flag came out, with only about twenty laps to go. This was going to be my best opportunity to win if I was going to because all the gaps were closed up. The green flag came out, and I felt like we were hungry wolves chasing the only piece of meat (a.k.a. the checkered flag) in California. I was driving around the outside of a car that decided to drift into me instead of lifting. That was it. That was the way I was going to end my season. Sixteen laps to go and nothing to show for it at Fontana.

March 8, 2006

Looking forward to 2006. Will it be better than 2005? Can you ever really beat the excitement of a breakout year? I am going to try with every fiber in my body. I was born to be a racecar driver, this I know. I live for the moments that I can hug my dad with relief or barbecue at the motor home with Mom, Dad, Brooke, and my husband. To me, life is what you make of it. I work really hard to please so many people, but at the end of the day, if you are not happy at home or with your family what do you have?

So I am going into the 2006 season not thinking about all the things I should do because it is year two. Lots of people think it should be a better year and some talk about a sophomore slump. I have to block it out.

This season, we have a different chassis from almost all the field now; we are sticking with the Panoz. It's one of those things we fought during every race last year. Also, everyone has a Honda engine. That was one of our advantages to some of the field last year and it's gone. There are also a few different rules for the car. It all creates new challenges. I am ready.

I must focus even more on racing because of all these new elements. I am going to make a commitment to not overload the schedule or lose the energy or edge I need to do what I was put here for—and that is to drive a racecar. I am going to make sure that I still keep having fun and enjoying life with those close to me, because that is what will make me fast. That is what will make me the best I can be!

Glossary

Aerodynamics. As applied to racing, the study of the interaction between air and the resistance and pressures created by a moving car passing through the air.

Air pressure. The amount of air (measured in pounds per cubic inch) in a tire; a critical component in the setup of a racecar.

Alternating red and yellow striped flag. Signals that oil, water, or some other substance on the track has made the surface slippery.

Back straight. The straightaway opposite the start-finish line located between turns 2 and 3 on an oval track; also known as the "backstretch."

Banking. A track's angle, measured from 0 degrees for a completely flat surface to 36 degrees for the most severe banking in the turns of some superspeedways.

Behind the wall. The area along the pit road that is located on the infield side of the small concrete wall adjacent to the pit boxes.

Glossary

Black flag. A flag waved at a specific car, either for a penalty or a mechanical problem, advising the driver that he or she must pit on the next lap and follow the instructions of the race officials.

Black flag with white cross. Signals that the driver has been disqualified from the event.

Blue flag with yellow diagonal stripe. The "passing flag," signaling slower cars to yield to faster traffic.

Braking traces. Computer-generated data that provides the driver and the team with information as to when and how hard a driver pushed the brakes at given points around the track.

Caution. A track condition, signaled by a yellow flag and/or light, that indicates trouble somewhere on the track. Drivers must slow down, not pass other cars, and follow a pace car during caution.

Chassis. The car frame or central body of the car. Also called the "tub."

Checkered flag. The flag indicating the end of a practice session, qualification attempt, or end of the race. At the end of the race, the checkered flag is first waved at the winner.

Closed-cockpit car. A racecar with a roof over the head of the driver.

Crew. Members of a race team who work on the car, either in the shop or at the track during a race weekend.

Crew chief. The day-to-day manager of the race team who oversees the mechanics and the crew. The crew chief, and in some cases the engineer, is the driver's primary contact, the person to whom the driver must relay all information about how the car is handling and feeling.

Differential. An axle gear assembly that regulates torque to each of the rear wheels.

Downforce. The downward pressure on the car created by air passing over the chassis and causing the car to grip the surface of the track. It keeps the car on the track. The wings of the car force it to stay on the ground, acting in a manner opposite to the wings on an airplane.

Drafting. A driving maneuver in which one or more cars line up single file behind the lead car, thus lengthening the airflow over the line of cars and cutting down on drag. Drafting allows the cars trailing the lead car to go faster using less horsepower. In a two-car situation, the lead car must accelerate to go fast. The second car can come out of the draft and slingshot past the first car with less acceleration. Drafting is also a common practice in cycling.

Drag. The resistance formed by the car passing through the air and creating turbulence around and behind it.

Glossary

Front stretch. The straight section of the racetrack where the start-finish line is located.

G-force. Gravitational force created by the high speed of the car as it makes turns on the track.

Go-kart. A small open-wheel racecar, typically with an engine and a frame but very little bodywork, used for entry-level as well as professional racing.

Green flag. Signals the start of the practice session, qualification attempt, or race, and all restarts after a caution or red flag.

Grip. Describes how well the tires maintain traction on the racing surface.

Groove (or line). The path around the track where cars run the fastest and handle the best. The groove of a track can shift several times during a race as conditions change. Often most drivers will use the same groove around the racetrack; that portion of the track will consequently appear darker due to the buildup of tire rubber.

Handling. A race car's on-track performance, determined by tire and suspension setup and other aerodynamic factors.

Horsepower (hp). a measurement of engine power.

Lap (noun). One time around the track.

Lap (verb). as in when a driver is "lapped."

Lapped. Being passed by another car so that it becomes one lap ahead.

Lap time. The time it takes for a car to make one lap, measured to the thousandth of a second.

Line. See Groove.

Marbles. Excessive rubber buildup above the groove of the track, the result of normal tire wear throughout a race.

Midget car. An open-wheel racecar often raced on dirt tracks.

Motocross bike. A form of motorcycle racing bike that is used primarily in off-track racing, typically on dirt with jumps and curves.

Nose. The front of a car.

Open-cockpit car. A racecar without a roof.

Open-wheel racing. Racing with cars that do not have fenders.

Oversteer. A condition where the rear end of the car is unstable due to lack of rear tire grip, also known as "loose."

Pit box. Area along the pit road just outside the pit wall where the car stops during pit stops.

Glossary

Pit crew. Seven members of the team designated to go into the pit box during a pit stop to work on the car.

Pit road or lane. The road connecting the track to the designated pit box area, usually located parallel to the front stretch.

Pit stall. Area behind the wall of the pit box where the tires and other equipment are kept and where the pit crew is stationed between pit stops.

Pit stop. Car's leaving the racetrack for service in the pit box.

Pit wall. The small concrete wall separating the pit box from the pit stall.

Podium. The stand or area where the top three drivers are presented with their trophies at the end of a race.

Points. Numerical values assigned by the IRL for wins, pole positions, finishing place, and leading the most laps. This numeric system determines the year-end champion.

Pole. The inside, front-row starting position, awarded to the car with the fastest qualifying time.

Racing suit. Fireproof suit worn by drivers any time they are in the car.

Red flag. The flag that tells all drivers to stop their cars at the end of the current lap; often brought out for serious accidents and rain.

Red flag with yellow "X." Signal that the pit area is closed.

Restart. The first green-flag lap after a caution; a critical strategic period for a team as most of the cars are close together and positions can be gained or lost depending on how aggressively the driver attacks the restart.

Road courses. Non-oval tracks with various turns, configurations, and elevation changes.

RPMs. Engine revolutions per minute.

Series. The races sanctioned by a specific racing organization during a calendar year.

Setup. The preparation of the car for a race including, but not limited to, the aerodynamics package, chassis position, stiffness of shocks and springs, and air pressure in the tires.

Side pod. Bodywork on the side of the chassis covering the radiators. Aids in engine cooling, car aerodynamics, and driver protection in the event of a side impact.

Speed traces. Computer-generated data that provides the driver and the team with acceleration and deceleration information at various points on the track.

Sponsors. Corporations and other entities that pay a team or driver money to have their logos and identities associated with them.

Spotter. The team member who watches the race from a perch above the track and radios to the driver when and where traffic is located, where to go to avoid an accident, or when the track has gone yellow or is about to go green.

Suspension. Shock absorbers and springs, similar to those on a regular car, but which are adjustable to smooth out bumps on the track and to maintain grip.

Sway bars. The bars that couple the suspensions on each side of the racecar to try to compress the springs on both sides of the car equally.

Team. All the employees and staff of a race organization assigned to a particular car.

Team manager. The big-picture manager inside a racing shop who handles everything from ordering parts to hiring and firing of personnel and coordinating test dates and times.

Understeer. Condition in which the car does not want to turn in the corners due to a lack of tire grip. This is also known as "pushing" or "tight."

White flag with red cross. Signal that an ambulance is on the course or that medical help is needed.

White line. A line on the inside of an oval track marking an area that should not be crossed during the race, except for entering and exiting pit road or in the event the car needs to slow down dramatically.

Wings. Aerodynamic fixtures generally on the front or rear of the car that help increase the downforce of the car.

Yellow flag. The caution flag that indicates trouble somewhere on the track. Drivers must slow down, maintain position, and yield to safety vehicles until the green flag is displayed. During a qualification session, a qualification attempt is halted.

Acknowledgments

I want to thank God for being there for me every step of the way, and for the gifts and talents I've been given, but most of all for my husband, family, and loved ones. Love is all you need.

Mom and Dad, without you I know for certain I would not be where I am today. You gave me everything I ever needed or wanted. "Thank you" will never be enough, but I'm going to keep saying it anyway . . . Thank you. I love you. The fun has just begun!

Brooke, seester, you are my biggest and best cheerleader. I know I can always talk to you and feel better about any situation. You are truly my best friend. I would do anything for you. Peace out. I love you.

Paul, you are my everything. You make me a better person. I have found real happiness with you. I know at the end of the day, it is you and me, and that is all I ever really need. I am so proud to be your wife for the rest of our lives. I love you. Your wifey!

Bob, you believed in me when no one else did and I will be forever grateful. It is because of that kind of support that little girl's dreams come true! Thank you from the bottom of my heart.

Dave, thank you for giving me the opportunity to show the world what I am made of! I am just glad that I can make you smile. Thank you.

Scott, you keep it all together, and I don't know how sometimes.

Acknowledgments

You are a wonderful man, with such a big heart. Thank you for making my job as your driver easier.

Ray, thank you for making me look like I was never a rookie. You are a calming and positive voice that I hope I have the good fortune of hearing for a long time.

Brent, what media outlet didn't you get a request from since Indy? You had a job that was bigger than anyone could have expected. It is because of you that I didn't go completely crazy at times. Thank you.

T.B., thank you for letting people know who Danica Patrick was before I was just "Danica." You helped open people's eyes. Thank you.

Jack, thank you for making me smile simply with your presence. I really do turn to you for advice on every decision I make. What would I have done without that for the last five years of my life.

Lynn, you arrived at a crucial time in my career. I would never be able to handle the business outside the car while driving at the same time. You let me do what I do best and that is being a racecar driver. Thank you.

Laura, thank you for your dedication and belief in this project. I know it has not been easy at times, but you heard my voice—put it on paper—and brought it to life! You pulled emotions and stories out of me that I never knew were there. You are a very gifted writer. And I have a feeling this is not the end.

Danica's family—Betty and Curtis Thompson, Joan and Greg Dahl, Harler and Sharon Flaten, Gary and Carla Flaten, Randy Patrick.

Paul's family—Joe and Louise, Mark and Mindy, Kurt and Denise, and Karl and Monica Hospenthal; Heidi and Marcus Spitzli.

My friends—Mary Ann, Marni, Heather, Stephie, TK, Kimmi, Tina, Amber, Merideth, Brock, Dan, Emily, Jarrett, Shondra, and Charity.

Sponsor and support—Wayne Lee, Sam Marzouk, and Mike Urtel at Argent; Robert Clarke at Honda; Bill and Jim Gerkin at Norwalk; Toni Birch at Bell Helmets; Joe Dorris at Futaba; Troy Lee Designs; Sparco USA; Pioneer; Steve Rosenberg at Kaenon; Amanda Ahmad and Casey Patterson at Spike TV; Run-Rite, Secret, Tissot, Old World Industries; Hostess; Mary Hamilton at BEBE; Mark Borchetta; Scott St. John; Brian Barnhart; Vicki O'Conner; Al Spire at Firestone; Hulman Family, Network Solutions.

Photography—Paul Webb, Brian Spurlock, Mike Levitt, Sutton Photography, Allen Mermelstein.

Past support—Mecom family, Lyn St. James, Tom Milner, Ford Racing.

Trident Media Group, Dan Strone, Lily, Kosner and to our awesome writer's assistant, Adam Mitchell—thanks for all of your help in making my book happen.

Simon & Schuster—My editor, Nancy Hancock, for her strong faith and belief in my story; her assistant, Sarah Peach; my publicists, Marcia Burch and Ellen Silberman; and the rest of the team—thanks for all of your work and dedication to my book.

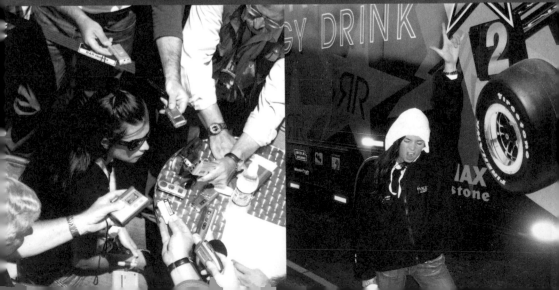